HEROES OF HISTORY

RONALD REAGAN

Destiny
at His Side

HEROES OF HISTORY

RONALD REAGAN

Destiny at His Side

JANET & GEOFF BENGE

Emerald
Books

P.O. BOX 635, LYNNWOOD, WA 98046

Emerald Books are distributed through YWAM Publishing. For a full list of titles, including other great biographies, visit our website at www.ywampublishing.com or call 1-800-922-2143.

Library of Congress Cataloging-in-Publication Data

Benge, Janet, 1958–
   Ronald Reagan : destiny at his side / By Janet and Geoff Benge.
      p. cm. — (Heroes of history)
   Includes bibliographical references.
   ISBN 978-1-932096-65-1 (pbk.)
1. Reagan, Ronald—Juvenile literature. 2. Presidents—United States—Biography—Juvenile literature. I. Benge, Geoff, 1954– II. Title.
   E877.B438 2010
   973.927092—dc22
   [B]   2010014214

Ronald Reagan: Destiny at His Side
Copyright © 2010 by Janet and Geoff Benge

14 13 12 11 10   1 2 3 4 5

Published by Emerald Books
P.O. Box 635
Lynnwood, Washington 98046

ISBN 978-1-932096-65-1

Printed in the United States of America.

HEROES OF HISTORY
Biographies

Abraham Lincoln
Alan Shepard
Benjamin Franklin
Christopher Columbus
Clara Barton
Daniel Boone
Douglas MacArthur
George Washington
George Washington Carver
Harriet Tubman
John Adams
John Smith
Laura Ingalls Wilder
Meriwether Lewis
Orville Wright
Ronald Reagan
Theodore Roosevelt
Thomas Edison
William Penn

More Heroes of History coming soon!
Unit study curriculum guides are available
for select biographies.

Available at your local bookstore or
through Emerald Books
1 (800) 922-2143

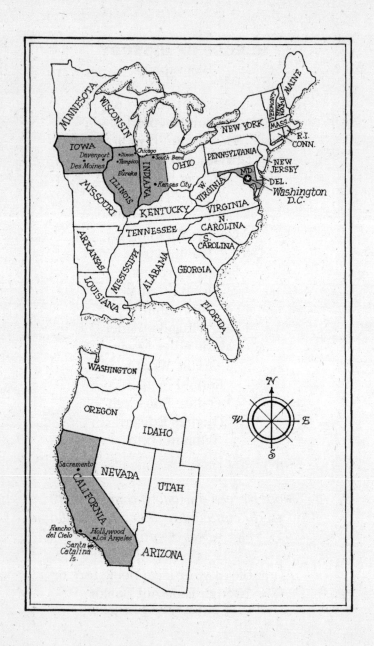

Contents

Chapter 1

"Get Us to GW!"

Pop! Pop! Pop! Pop! Pop! Pop! The sound of the gunshots came in quick succession.

Startled, Ron stopped waving to the small crowd that cheered him as he emerged onto T Street from the Washington Hilton Hotel. "What's that?" he asked Secret Service Agent Jerry Parr, though he was certain it had been gunshots.

Jerry Parr did not answer. Instead, to Ron's astonishment, the Secret Service agent tackled him. Just as Ron was about to go down, another agent rushed over and pushed both Ron and Jerry into the back of the presidential limousine. Ron could hear shouts of "Get him out! Get him out!" as he hit the floor of the limousine. The door slammed shut behind him.

"Take off!" Jerry yelled, and the limousine sped away.

An excruciating pain shot down Ron's left side. "Get off me, Jerry," he said. "I think you've broken one of my ribs."

The two men disentangled from each other and climbed onto the back seat of the limousine. Jerry ran his hands down Ron's back and side. "No blood," he said, indicating that the president appeared not to have been hit by a bullet.

Suddenly, as if on cue, Ron coughed, and bright red blood frothed out of his mouth. Ron wiped the blood away with his handkerchief. "I think I've cut my mouth as well," he said.

Jerry took one look at Ron and yelled to the driver, "Get us to GW!"

The limousine swerved into a side street and roared off toward George Washington University Hospital five blocks away. Ron tried to take a breath—a shallow breath so as not to jar his ribcage—but he could not get air into his lungs. He sat up straight and tried again. "I can't breathe," he finally gasped as a wave of panic swept over him.

Ron struggled to understand what was happening. It wasn't supposed to be like this. He had been president of the United States for a little over two months and had so many things he wanted to accomplish. Now he was being rushed to the hospital in the back of a limousine, unable to breathe, with searing pain in his side.

Moments later the limousine screeched to a halt outside the emergency room. Jerry opened the car door and said, "I'll get a gurney."

"No," Ron replied, "I'll walk in." With that, he swung his legs around, stood up, and leaned on

Jerry's arm. Together they walked the twenty feet to the emergency room entrance. The automatic doors swung open just as Ron collapsed onto one knee. He desperately tried to gasp for another breath. He could feel himself becoming weak and lightheaded, but there was nothing he could do. Then he felt himself being lifted onto a gurney. As his body was placed on the gurney, Ron wondered if this was how it was going to end for the boy from rural Illinois. Things like this had never happened back in Dixon.

Dutch

Five-year-old Ronald "Dutch" Reagan lay on the floor, a newspaper spread in front of him. He looked closely at the photograph on the front page that showed an aerial view of a parade stopped midroute. Dutch could see a marching band at the edge of the photo.

Overcome with curiosity at what the photo could be of, Dutch peered at the squiggly black lines beneath the photograph. Suddenly, as if the squiggles were tiny tin soldiers marshalling themselves, the lines turned into words in his head. Ron strung the words together and said them silently: "...such events as the aftermath of a bomb that had exploded in San Francisco during a parade."

"What are you doing?" Dutch's father, Jack Reagan, asked.

"Reading," Dutch replied.

His father laughed, but his mother, Nelle Reagan, rushed across the room and leaned over the newspaper.

Dutch said the words aloud.

"Dutch, did you just read that?" his mother asked.

Dutch nodded. He guessed that he had.

"I don't think so," his father interjected as he stretched his neck to look at his younger son. "The lad can't read. He's only been going to school for a few months, and those are big words."

"Well, it seems to me like he can," Nelle replied. "Read some more, Dutch."

Dutch looked down at the newspaper, hoping that the squiggles would continue to untangle themselves for him, and they did: "...and the exciting details of the two-dead, Black Tom explosion in New Jersey."

"He *is* reading!" Dutch's mother exclaimed as she stood to rush out the door.

Minutes later she reappeared in the room with several neighbors, who were also astonished at Dutch's newfound ability.

"How'd he do it?" one of the neighbors asked Nelle. "Those aren't words you learn in first grade."

"Well, I do read to the boys every night, and I run my fingers under the words so that they can follow along. I guess Dutch just followed along more closely than I ever imagined. He must have taught himself from just watching me!"

In fact, that *is* what had happened. From that time on, Dutch was able to read the newspaper for himself, though he did not understand a lot of what he read.

In 1916 many adults were finding it difficult to comprehend what was happening in the United States and the rest of the world. Germany, under the leadership of Kaiser Wilhelm, was at war with the rest of Europe, and people in the United States were divided about whether or not Americans should go to Europe's aid. This led to many violent protests, including the parade bombing in San Francisco, where a suitcase bomb had exploded during a war preparedness parade, killing ten people.

This event was the first thing Dutch had ever read about to himself. Dutch asked his father many questions about the Great War, as the war in Europe was called, and his father told him as much as he could.

In April 1917 the United States declared war on Germany and entered the Great War in Europe. Soon soldiers were being shipped out to the muddy battlefields of France to reinforce the British, the French, and their allies in the war against Germany. Dutch read about some of this in the newspaper, but he much preferred to read *The Boys' Annual* and adventure stories about people lost in Alaska or even about outer space. He wanted to learn all he could about the world, which was a challenge for a five-year-old living in the western Illinois town of Galesburg.

The Reagan family had moved numerous times since Dutch's birth on February 6, 1911, in Tampico, Illinois. By 1918 the family moved yet again, but this was the first move where Dutch was fully aware that he was leaving one place and starting over again somewhere different. While the city of Monmouth was only sixteen miles away, the move meant a whole new life for a six-year-old boy. Dutch had to start attending another public school and Sunday school, where he had to make new friends.

Central School was an eye-opening experience for Dutch, who was shy and far ahead of his class with his reading. These two things made it hard for him to make new friends. There was one other thing that Dutch did not quite understand. Because he had an Irish surname—Reagan—and his father, Jack Reagan, spent a lot of time at the local pub, everyone assumed that Dutch was Catholic. And he was—sort of. Although Dutch attended the local Disciples of Christ church, a Protestant denomination his mother's English side of the family adhered to, his father and all of his family were Catholics. In fact, Dutch had been baptized as an infant in the Catholic Church, but he had rarely ever attended services there.

In 1918 there was much prejudice against Catholics, especially in small, isolated, rural towns like Monmouth. After only one week of school, Dutch found himself the target of a bunch of bullies, led by a girl named Gertie.

Dutch knew nothing about the group until he noticed that he was being tailed by a couple of girls. Then a group of boys joined the girls, and together they started taunting Dutch. Being small for his age and outnumbered, Dutch decided to make a run for it. He bolted toward his house on South Seventh Street, the other children in pursuit. He was able to outrun the group, and he yelled for his mother to help him. Nelle Reagan appeared on the porch and immediately knew what was happening. Although she was a petite woman, she pulled herself up to her full height and gave the bullies a lecture on Christian charity and kindness to strangers. The group sheepishly and quickly backed away.

Things at school were a little easier for Dutch after that, and living on Seventh Street had its advantages. Seventh Street was just one block off Main Street, and the Great War had reached a feverish pitch. Almost every month there was some kind of war-related parade. Bands played, speeches were made, and even effigies (models) of Kaiser Wilhelm were burned right in the street.

Dutch's mother allowed Dutch and his older brother, Neil, to go to the parades alone, as did many of the parents of other children in his class. Sometimes Dutch and Neil would visit their father at the E. B. Colwell Department Store on South Main Street. It was a fancy store with a doorman and row upon row of merchandise lining the shelves around the walls. Men in suits attended to the customers. Jack Reagan was one of these men. He worked in the shoe department, and even before they saw him, Dutch and Neil could hear his deep laugh. Jack loved to tell stories and jokes to his customers and often admired the "turn of a lady's ankle."

Dutch's chest swelled with pride as he saw his father laughing with a customer. No one was more fun to be around than Jack Reagan—when he was happy. However, Jack had another side, a side that Dutch did not like to think about much, a side that came out when his father drank too much alcohol. Sometimes Dutch overheard his mother pleading with his father to give up drinking. He knew that the drinking was the real reason the family moved around so much. It was not new opportunities his father was looking for. Rather, the family moved because Jack Reagan had been fired from his last job for being drunk.

Because he felt like he was beginning to fit in, Dutch hoped that his father would keep the job in Monmouth. But it was not his father's drinking that turned out to be the next challenge for the family. In November 1918 the Great War ended and celebrations were held all over the United States. School was canceled, and Dutch watched the victory parade with delight. Within days, however, another enemy had taken over—the great flu epidemic.

The epidemic was worldwide, and when it reached Monmouth, millions of people around the globe had died from the flu. With the onset of the epidemic, Monmouth's schools were closed to slow the spread of the disease, and everyone wore a mask over his or her mouth. Even these precautions did not keep Nelle Reagan from coming down with influenza. It was a somber time for seven-year-old Dutch as he watched Dr. Laurence visit his mother. The doctor carried a large, black leather bag, and every time he left, Dutch's father would say, "He says Nelle's going to be all right." Dutch could tell from the tone of his father's voice that his father did not really believe the doctor.

The days dragged on. There was little to do, since everyone was told to stay away from each other as much as possible. A person could catch the flu just going to the store or talking to someone outside the gate. One day, Jack told Dutch that his mother was going to be all right, and this time Dutch could see from the smile on his father's face that he really meant it. His mother was not going to die after all.

Soon after receiving the good news about his mother's improved condition, Dutch himself got sick, not with the flu, but with pneumonia. Although it was not the flu, it was still a serious illness, one from which children and elderly people often died. Once again Dr. Laurence began making regular trips to the Reagan home, prescribing treatments and medicines for Dutch. Dutch had to stay in bed for weeks while he recovered.

No sooner had Dutch recovered from pneumonia than another member of the family needed medical attention. This time it was his brother Neil, who was hit by a truck and suffered a broken leg.

All of these situations, plus the cost of Jack Reagan's alcohol, put a severe strain on the family budget. The medical bills piled up, and Dutch's mother prayed for a way out of debt. The answer to her prayers came in the form of a new job offer for Jack—a job with higher pay and even the possibility of becoming a partner in a general store. Jack accepted the offer, and in August 1919 the family moved back to Tampico, Illinois, where Dutch had been born. In Tampico Jack went back to work with his former boss, H. C. Pitney.

Dutch loved his new life in Tampico. The family rented an apartment right at the top of the Pitney store on Main Street, and it seemed to Dutch like the whole world paraded past their house. At night he and Neil would sit at the bottom of the steps that led up to their apartment, eating popcorn and chatting with everyone who walked by.

Sometimes Dutch would walk with his mother past the Graham Building, where he had been born. The apartment they had been living in at the time was on the second floor, and his mother would point out the outhouse they used when they lived there. The outhouse was down the stairs and behind the building. Dutch's mother told him that the apartment had three stoves for heating, but it had been quite an effort for her to carry all that coal up the stairs. Dutch wanted to ask why his father didn't carry the coal upstairs, but he knew that most of the work around the house fell to his mother.

Sometimes as they walked past the old apartment building, Nelle would tell Dutch about the day he was born. It was during one of the worst snowstorms in memory, and the roads were impassable. Because Nelle's labor was going badly, Jack braved the storm to fetch the doctor. The doctor was out on another call, and Jack trudged on to find the midwife. The midwife had already delivered the baby when the doctor made it to the apartment. "For such a little bit of a Dutchman, he makes a heck of a lot of noise, doesn't he?" the doctor joked.

Jack looked at the newly born ten-pound baby, Ronald Wilson Reagan. (Wilson was Ronald's mother's maiden name.) His hair was blond and his eyes blue. His father decided that he was as fat as one of the little Dutch boy figurines he had seen pictured in magazines. "He does look like a Dutchman," Jack agreed. And the name stuck. Instead of being called Ronald or Ron, from that day on he was called Dutch by all who knew him. Dutch always loved hearing the story of his birth and how he got his name, and his mother always seemed happy to tell it to him.

All in all, Dutch thought that his mother seemed happier about a lot of things now that the family had returned to Tampico. Nelle had joined the local theater group, and, of course, she quickly became an active member of the local church.

Harold Winchell, or "Monkey," as everyone called him, lived across the street from the Reagans. Monkey's dad owned a shoe shop, and the Winchell family lived in the apartment above the store. Like Dutch's father, Monkey's dad liked to hunt. But whereas Jack Reagan had a single-shot shotgun, Monkey's dad had a five-shot shotgun. And Dutch had to see the weapon for himself. One day while Dutch was visiting Monkey, the boys pulled out the five-shot shotgun to check it out. With the butt of the gun on the floor and the barrel pointed straight up toward the ceiling, the shotgun was taller than either of the boys.

Eventually Dutch's curiosity got the better of him, and he pulled the trigger. The gun did nothing more than make a click. Then Monkey pumped the shotgun. This time when Dutch pulled the trigger, the gun let out a deafening boom as buckshot burst from the barrel and went straight through the ceiling. Chunks of plaster and dust rained down on the two boys, who stood in stunned silence. Moments later the boys heard footsteps running up the stairs. Dutch quickly laid down the shotgun, and he and Monkey dove for the couch. When the door to the room burst open, Dutch and Monkey were sitting quietly side by side reading a copy of the *Sunday School Quarterly.* As the adults entered the room, despite the fact that the room was filled with plaster dust, Dutch looked up and smiled, as if to say, "What's the problem? We're just reading."

Jack was not impressed with his son's behavior and quickly administered punishment in the form of a whipping. When it was over, Dutch assured himself that he was going to be more careful the next time he pulled the trigger of a shotgun.

Not long after the incident with the shotgun, Jack came home one day and told his two sons that he had bought a boxcar full of potatoes. The potatoes could not be sold to a store because some of them were rotten. Dutch and Neil, Jack announced, were to separate the rotten potatoes from the good ones.

The task proved to be the worst experience of Dutch's young life, far worse than any whipping he could have received from his father. The boxcar was pulled onto a railway siding. As their father slid open the boxcar door, the stench of rotten potatoes hit the boys. Dutch gagged, but his father made him climb up on top of the pile and start sorting.

Dutch picked up a graying potato, which dissolved in his hand as putrid slime ran down his wrist. He threw the rotting potato into a sack his father had handed him and then picked up the next potato. By the end of the day, the two brothers reeked of rotten potatoes, and Dutch prayed that they would not run into anyone they knew on the way home. To make matters worse, Nelle had the boys bring home the good potatoes, which appeared in various forms at every meal.

Day after day, Neil and Dutch were sent back to the boxcar to continue the unpleasant job of sorting the potatoes. With each passing day, the effect of the sun heating the boxcar made conditions inside less bearable. Soon the boys could stand it no longer. They dumped the remainder of the potatoes, whether they were good or rotten, and told their father that they had completed the job. Despite his Irish ancestry, Dutch knew that he would never enjoy eating another potato as long as he lived!

Somehow the Reagan family managed to struggle along. The postwar prosperity that the newspapers talked about did not seem to hit Midwestern farmers, and most families around Tampico struggled to make ends meet, as did the Reagans.

Dutch took comfort in knowing that he was not the only kid at school who put cardboard inside the bottom of his boots when the soles wore through or wore his older brother's hand-me-downs.

Some of the best things about life in Tampico could not be bought. They were free, such as spending the summer swimming in the ditches to the north of town or riding a borrowed bike or being rewarded for raking up leaves in the school yard with a big marshmallow roast.

These things were all fun, but the thing that Dutch enjoyed most of all was watching the Saturday movie matinees at the local opera house. A different Western feature played nearly every Saturday afternoon, and Dutch carried coal for the boilers at the opera house in exchange for free admission to the movie. As far as he was concerned, it was the best deal he ever made. Dutch always sat in the front row, his imagination fired up by the Western and the pounding of the opera house piano, which provided the musical soundtrack for the silent movie.

Modern movie technology was a marvel to Dutch, but nothing compared to the new device he would soon discover.

Chapter 3

Dixon

Dutch loved Christmastime, and he loved to see new things, so he especially loved Christmas 1919. His mother had saved a little money from making some sewing alterations for the Pitney store. She had enough to buy four train tickets to her Wilson relatives' farm near Morrison, Illinois.

The whole trip was an adventure. A snowstorm had blown in from the north. Dutch peered out the train window watching the falling snow swirl in the wind before settling to the ground. At the train station in Morrison, the Reagans were met by their relatives and whisked away in an open sleigh. Dutch was tucked under a buffalo skin blanket and told to place his feet on hot bricks that had been laid on the floor of the sleigh to keep him warm. Soon they were making their way through snowdrifts toward the Wilson farm.

At the farm, the family was welcomed into the large farmhouse and served bowls of steaming hot soup. Dutch especially liked the idea that he could have a second bowl of soup if he wanted. And while he appreciated the abundance of food that he was served during the family's stay at the farm, what Dutch liked most about the time was listening to the small crystal set radio. Dutch pulled the headphones over his ears and listened as a faint voice announced, "This is KDKA, Pittsburgh." Then he listened to some scratchy music coming to him across the airway. Dutch could hardly believe what he was hearing. It was almost like magic. Radio waves somehow passed silently through the air from Pittsburg, until they found the little crystal set in his relatives' farmhouse that was somehow able to turn the waves into the sound of a voice and musical instruments that could be heard through headphones. Dutch wished he knew exactly how it all worked. Nonetheless, he was happy to sit and listen to the radio through the headphones. When he had finished listening, he would put down the headphones and mimic the announcer he had heard talking. "This is KDKA, Pittsburgh," he would say, trying to put a manly inflection into his young voice.

Once Christmas was over, what with all the food to eat and the crystal set radio to listen to, Dutch found it hard to leave the Wilson farm and return to Tampico. Back home, things were not going well with his father, who got drunk almost every Saturday night. Nelle tried hard to keep things in the family as normal as possible, but sometimes Dutch would see his mother on her knees praying five or six times a day that her husband would manage to stay sober for a whole weekend. This never happened, though the U.S. government was about to do everything it could to help out Nelle and others like her.

On January 16, 1920, the Eighteenth Amendment to the U.S. Constitution went into effect. This amendment banned the sale, manufacture, and transportation of alcohol within the United States. The period known as Prohibition had begun. The only bar in Tampico closed, and overnight Dutch's father had nowhere to go and drink. However, he soon worked out a solution to the problem. A drink called "near beer" was still available for sale. This drink was, in fact, beer that had had its alcohol content siphoned off before being bottled. It tasted like real beer but contained no alcohol. Jack began buying medicinal alcohol from the drugstore, which he would add to the near beer to return it to its former alcohol-laden state so that he could get drunk. It was not whiskey, his drink of choice, but it satisfied his addiction to alcohol.

Another problem that arose from the closure of the only saloon in town was not so easy for Jack to solve. Jack now had nowhere to go at night, nowhere to socialize with other men and entertain them with his stories. Dutch's mother suggested that he start attending prayer meetings with her, but he was not interested. Instead, he became bored and depressed.

For his part, Dutch tried to get away from the house when things got unpleasant at home. He loved to play football with his friends and read books at the local library. Then there was the ultimate escape—movies at the Saturday matinee at the opera house.

In December 1920, sixteen months after moving back to Tampico with high hopes, the Reagans were packing up to leave again. This time it was because H. C. Pitney had sold his store. He had promised to give Jack some of the proceeds from the sale but changed his mind at the last moment. Instead, Pitney offered Jack part ownership in another business, the Fashion Boot Shop, located twenty-six miles away in Dixon, Illinois.

By the time Jack had finished describing the place, Dutch and Neil were excited to be moving there. Dixon's population was about eight thousand people, making it a much larger place than Tampico. Dixon was big enough for the circus to come to town once a year and for the school to have a winning football team. Jack promised his sons that he would rent a house with a yard for them to play in. He also bought an old car from Pitney so the family could take excursions into the countryside beyond Dixon.

On December 6, 1920, the family piled all of their possessions on top of the car and headed for their new home. Onboard were four stowaways: Dutch's cat Guinevere and her three kittens, King Arthur, Sir Galahad, and Buster. Dutch's father had forbidden the boys to bring the cats, but Nelle had smuggled them under the back seat. Dutch hoped that the cats would not give themselves away by meowing before they got to their new home. Thankfully the cats were silent all the way until the car pulled up in front of South 816 Hennepin Avenue.

The place reminded Dutch of a gingerbread house, with its high-pitched roof and overlapping clapboard siding. When Dutch explored the new house, he discovered that it was smaller inside than it appeared from the outside. Three tiny bedrooms were upstairs: one for his parents, one to be used as a sewing room so that his mother could make a little extra money, and a bedroom for the boys. Since only one twin bed would fit into that room, Dutch and Neil had to share it.

It didn't matter much to Dutch how small the interior of the house was. Something far better was beckoning him in the backyard, where a barn twenty-four feet long and fourteen feet wide sat. The barn was rundown, for sure, but it had a loft that Jack Reagan said the boys could use as their den. Dutch and Neil dreamed up all sorts of things they could do in the barn, just as soon as they made friends with some of the local boys.

Making friends, however, took a little time for Dutch, who was now in fifth grade. Dutch was still shy, and although he was a good student, he was sure that he had to concentrate harder than the other children to get high grades. Finally, though, he did make friends with other boys, including George and Ed O'Malley, who lived across the street from the Reagans. George was the same age as Neil, and Ed was Dutch's age. The boys liked to get together and play football, the two older boys against the younger two.

Dutch liked his new life in Dixon. His father had been right—there was so much more to do in Dixon than in Tampico. The swift-flowing Rock River ran through the middle of town, and it was said that the best catfish in America could be caught in its waters. And there was Lowell Park, where in the summer you could swim, go boating, and fish. The town also had many more stores than Tampico, and on Saturday nights it seemed like everybody in Dixon headed for the heart of town to spend the evening.

Dutch was also delighted when his parents let him have his own dog, a Boston terrier named Bobby Jiggs. Dutch and the dog had lots of fun together. Bobby Jiggs had a lot of energy, and Dutch came up with a game to help burn off some of it. Behind the house and beyond the barn, the back lawn sloped downhill. Dutch would tie a stick to the end of a fishing line, stand at the top of the slope, and cast the fishing line—with the stick on the end—to the bottom of the slope. Bobby Jiggs would bound after the stick, and when the stick was firmly in the dog's mouth, Dutch would reel him in with the fishing line. The two of them would spend hours passing the time.

As summer rolled around, Dutch had developed a network of friends. Together the boys spent many hours at Lowell Park swimming and boating. The current in the Rock River was strong there, and swimmers often got into difficulty and occasionally drowned. But Dutch knew that his mother would not worry about him. He was a stronger swimmer than most grown men.

One day during summer, Jack brought an old display case home from the shoe store. Dutch installed the case in the loft of the barn and set about filling it with birds' eggs, which he eagerly climbed trees to collect. Neil went a step further. He trapped young pigeons and squirrels and kept them in cages in the loft. On Saturday mornings he would kill the pigeons and squirrels, then skin and clean them. Neil would then put them in a basket and go door-to-door throughout the neighborhood selling the pigeons and squirrels to people to cook for their Saturday dinners. Dutch would have liked the extra money Neil got from doing this, but he could not bring himself to kill animals the way his brother did.

Dutch also joined the local library and began reading two books a week from its shelves. His choices included the *Tarzan* and *Frank Merriwell* series of books, but he liked Westerns most of all.

Nelle loved movies as much as Dutch, and the family normally went to the movies together on Friday night at the Dixon Theater. Then, if Dutch timed his asking right, his father would give him a penny to go again the next day to see the Saturday matinee.

The movies exposed Dutch to many new places and ideas. Most of the time Dutch's parents let him watch whatever he chose, but Jack drew the line when Dutch wanted to see a movie sympathetic to the Ku Klux Klan. Dutch's father told him that any man who hid under a sheet while making life miserable for a fellow human being was a bum, and there was no way he was going to let his son watch such a movie.

Dutch did not see the movie, but his father's words got him thinking about why people, such as those in the Ku Klux Klan, hated black people. He could not understand why. Black children went to his school, and black and white adults ate at the same lunch counters and attended the movie theater together. In fact, one of Dutch's best friends was a black boy named Wink. The two of them played football together, and Wink often came over to the Reagan house after school to play. Dutch's mother encouraged Dutch to get to know all people, regardless of race. Equality was at the heart of her religious beliefs.

In truth, Nelle's beliefs influenced Dutch in many ways. Nelle was a firm believer that God was watching over their family and keeping them safe no matter how difficult things became. Sometimes when money was especially tight, the family would take in a boarder or Nelle would sew through the night making alterations to the clothes of richer folk. No matter what happened, she gave ten percent of all she earned to the First Christian Church in Dixon, and she insisted that the boys do the same.

Sometimes Dutch would complain about this not being fair, but his mother would counter with, "The Lord will make your ninety percent twice as large if you make sure He gets His tenth first!"

While Nelle was able to influence her sons to do the right thing by the Lord, she did not make much headway with her husband. Even during Prohibition, Jack found ways to get drunk most Saturday nights. One evening, as Dutch was returning home, he almost tripped over something by the doorstep. As he looked down, Dutch saw his father passed out on his back, his arms outstretched. Dutch bent down to try to wake his father and immediately smelled the odor of alcohol. Since his mother was not home at the time, Dutch decided to take matters into his own hands. He grabbed his father by his coat and dragged him inside to the bedroom. It was a Herculean effort, but somehow he managed to get his unconscious father into bed. He never told his mother about the incident.

Around this time, Dutch read a book titled *That Printer of Udell's* by Harold Bell Wright. The novel tells the story of a man named Dick, whose father had killed his mother during a drunken rage. In the course of the story, Dick goes through a series of difficult situations until he reaches out to God, who helps him to turn his life around. At the end of the book, the main character decides to become a congressman so that he can do the most good for the most people.

Reading *That Printer of Udell's* had a profound influence on Dutch, who spent a lot of time thinking about the direction in which he wanted his life to go. Soon he approached his mother and announced that he wanted to follow God and be baptized. On June 21, 1922, Dutch and Neil Reagan were baptized together at the First Christian Church in Dixon, Illinois. After the baptism, things continued pretty much as they had before for Dutch, only now he taught a Sunday school class at church for younger boys, and he attended more prayer meetings.

Around this time a popular comic strip began appearing regularly in the newspaper. The comic strip featured a character named Moon Mullins, who sported the same slicked-back hair as Neil Reagan. Fairly soon afterward people began calling Neil "Moon." In fact, from that time on Neil was hardly ever called by his real name. Just as Ronald Reagan was known as Dutch, Neil Reagan was now known as Moon.

After his baptism, Dutch became more active in the Chautauqua events that were held at Lowell Park for two weeks during the summer. Chautauqua was named after a town in New York State where the original event was held. Basically the event consisted of a mix of Christian lectures and sermons along with appearances by various visiting people who spoke on cultural topics or demonstrated the latest in scientific breakthroughs and the like. Many people would come to Dixon to stay for the two weeks of the event. They camped out in Lowell Park, and the whole place took on a fair-like atmosphere that Dutch loved.

One afternoon on a trip to Lowell Park to attend the Chautauqua, a man named Louis Williams, who billed himself as an electrical entertainer, was giving a demonstration. Dutch decided to attend the demonstration. As he liked to do, he sat as close to the speaker as possible to take everything in. What Dutch saw captivated his imagination as Louis Williams used electric current to do all sorts of amazing things. Dutch thought about how wonderful it would be to be an electrical demonstrator, traveling the country, educating and entertaining large crowds. But in the summer of 1923, that kind of life seemed about as far from Dixon, Illinois, as a person could get.

Chapter 4

Lifeguard

One late winter day in 1924, the Reagan family were taking a Sunday afternoon drive. They often took such drives at the beginning of the month, because as the month wore on, they often had no more money for gasoline.

As they drove along, Moon began to read the advertising signs at the side of the road. Some of the things he read were funny, and Jack made up little ditties about them. Dutch frowned as he peered out the car window. A thought struck him as he noticed something: Moon could read the signs, but he could not. The signs were simply a blur.

On a whim, Dutch asked his mother if he could borrow her glasses for a minute. She handed them over, and when Dutch put them on, something magical happened. A whole new world came into focus! For the first time ever, Dutch could see the skyline clearly, with its bare trees and wintry sun sinking toward the horizon. He could also read the signs along the roadside. Better yet, when he asked his mother to hand him a map from under the front seat, he could see every detail on it.

It was hard to believe, but that day the Reagan family realized that Dutch had very poor eyesight. No wonder he always sat in the front row at school and church, and no wonder he loved playing football but not baseball. He was never able to see something as small as a baseball coming toward him.

The next day Nelle took Dutch straight to the optician, who fitted him with a pair of huge black-rimmed glasses. They were the fashion of the day, but Dutch thought they made him look odd. And although he loved to see things clearly, Dutch hated to be seen in public wearing his glasses. To add to his woes about how he looked, Dutch was now thirteen years old and was still small for his age. He wondered whether he would ever have a growth spurt like some of the other boys in his class.

The previous summer, the family had moved to a cheaper house at 338 West Everett Street in Dixon. While the rent was definitely lower, as Jack Reagan said, "You get what you pay for." And what the family got for their money wasn't much. The house had only one bedroom, so Dutch and Moon slept out on the screened porch. Most of all, though, Dutch missed the decaying barn at the back of the old house. He missed climbing up to its loft and sorting through the nature collection that he kept in the old display case his father had brought home.

The Reagan family had taken other measures to save money. When Nelle went to the butcher, she always asked for liver for the cats. The butcher did not charge for a little cat food. However, the liver was not really for the cats, who were happy eating the mice they caught. Instead, the Reagan family ate the liver at least once a week, and oatmeal meat became one of Dutch's favorite foods. Nelle mixed ground beef with an equal part of oatmeal and made meatloaf or meatballs with the mixture. Although his mother struggled to put food on the table, Dutch knew she was always looking out for those who were less fortunate than they were. On many occasions Nelle made a second meal for a family that she knew would go hungry without her help.

Because the new house was located on the north side of town, Dutch entered ninth grade at the North Campus of Dixon High School while Moon continued to go to the South Campus of Dixon High. However, both campuses had the same sports teams.

While small for a ninth grader, now that he wore glasses, Dutch was able to see everything the other students saw, and he made even better grades than before. Despite his academic progress, Dutch longed to be on the high school football team. His brother Neil was already a star on the team, and Dutch thought that one day he could be also. He began showing up for practice to try out for the team. Since he was only five feet three inches tall and weighed only 108 pounds, there wasn't even a team uniform small enough to fit him, except for a pair of pants that were still baggy on him. Nonetheless, Dutch gave it his best shot, but he was just too small, and the football coach chose bigger players to be on the team that year.

Despite not making the high school football team, Dutch would lie in bed at night and run over plays in his mind. He might not have made the team that year, but he was determined, and when he finally did make it, he'd be the most prepared player in the history of Dixon High School.

Although Dutch did well academically, his father discouraged him from even imagining that he could ever go on to university. At the time, only seven out of one hundred students who graduated from high school went on to college, and as Jack put it bluntly to his son, "Poor kids don't go to college."

Still, something within Dutch made him determined to improve himself. On weekends and after school he worked at any odd jobs he could find. One of his favorite jobs was as a circus helper when the Ringling Brothers Circus came to town. Dutch earned twenty-five cents an hour doing whatever needed to be done, from feeding the elephants to helping to pitch the big-top tent for circus performances.

The job Dutch found for the summer of 1925, however, was not as much fun as being a roustabout for the circus. Dutch was hired to work for a building contractor. He was paid thirty-five cents an hour to dig trenches with a pick and shovel for drains and foundations. As the summer progressed, the contractor allowed him to do some more interesting work, including pouring concrete, laying floors, and erecting roofs. Although it was hard, physical work for a fourteen-year-old boy, Dutch found that he loved to work with his hands and learn new skills. He gave ten percent of what he earned to the church and banked the rest of the money. One way or another, Dutch was determined to earn enough money during his remaining years of high school so that he could go to college.

Dutch returned to school for tenth grade with newfound muscle, though he had not grown much taller. However, that year the football conference added a new division for boys weighing less than 135 pounds. Dutch became Dixon High School's most enthusiastic new football player, and he was soon elected captain of the team.

Dutch continued to earn money from after-school jobs. This gave him the money he needed to join the YMCA, where he participated in the supervised swimming program and eventually passed the lifeguard test. Even though he was not the oldest or the biggest boy in the group, Dutch was by far the best swimmer. The swimming coach encouraged him and helped him to perfect his style. This training proved useful to Dutch as time went on.

In the spring of 1926, when Dutch was fifteen years old, several drownings occurred at Lowell Park. Dutch could understand why the Park Commission threatened to close the park to the public unless something could be done to make it safer for swimmers, but the thought of the park being closed horrified him. Lowell Park was the main source of summer fun for the children of Dixon. What would they do without it?

Dutch came up with an idea. He went to the park concessionaires, Ruth and Ed Graybill, and suggested that they hire him as a lifeguard at the park. At first the Graybills laughed at the idea of giving a fifteen-year-old boy such a responsibility, but after much persuasion they agreed to give Dutch a chance. The first day that he showed up for work at his new job as a lifeguard, Dutch knew that it was the summer job for him. He got to be outside all day long near the water, ready to dive in at a moment's notice and save somebody. Not only that, Dutch was paid eighteen dollars a week for doing something he loved to do, and he was allowed to consume all the nickel root beers and ten-cent hamburgers he wanted from the Graybills' concession stand.

Sometimes in the morning Dutch would give swimming lessons to the small children. In the afternoon he would joke around with some of his school friends who had come to hang out at the park. Yet he never forgot that he was there to be vigilant; the lives of people depended upon his vigilance. Although Dutch had to rescue a number of people who got into trouble in the swift current of the Rock River, no one drowned that summer. Dutch kept a tally of the people he rescued by carving notches into an old tree trunk.

In the fall Dutch entered his junior year at Dixon High School. During the previous year he had experienced the growth spurt he had been hoping for. He was now six feet tall and weighed 160 pounds. He played football and basketball and ran track. In football he was elevated to play for the high school's top team, but he found himself often warming the bench, watching the game from the sidelines and waiting to be called upon to play. Dutch also liked any kind of theater production and performed in school plays. He also wrote and illustrated for the high school yearbook. In short, Dutch was very busy.

One other activity took up a lot of Dutch's time that year—dating Margaret Cleaver. Margaret was a petite, auburn-haired girl who was in Dutch's class at high school and in the Christian Endeavor group he attended. Her father was pastor of the Dixon Christian Church, and Dutch had already spent many hours staring at Margaret in church on Sundays. In eleventh grade he got up the courage to ask Margaret out.

Since he worked at Lowell Park as a lifeguard, Dutch had access to a canoe. For a date, Dutch would often take Margaret out in the canoe on the Rock River. To enliven the atmosphere, he would bring along a portable windup Victrola, on which he would play records. He and Margaret would float in the canoe and talk and listen to music together.

Meanwhile, Dutch's brother Moon had graduated from high school and taken a job as a job-cost estimator at the Medusa Portland Cement Company. Dutch knew that his father was relieved to have at least one of his sons earning a full-time wage, though his mother was disappointed that Moon had not gone on to college. Her disappointment was compounded when Moon announced that he was changing his Christian allegiance to the local Catholic church. It felt to Dutch like the family had split in two. One half, his father and brother, were Catholics and did not seem to value higher education, while the other half, Dutch and his mother, were Protestants with dreams of Dutch attending college.

During his senior year, Dutch was busier than ever. In addition to engaging in his usual sports and acting activities, he was voted class president. And perhaps even more important, he became involved in politics for the first time.

Jack Reagan was a staunch Democrat, and the 1928 presidential campaign was approaching. Herbert Hoover was the Republican candidate for president, and Al Smith was the Democratic candidate. Al Smith was the governor of New York and known as a man of decisive action. He was also a Catholic. For these reasons Jack threw his support behind Smith. Soon the family car was emblazoned with Al Smith banners, and Jack did all he could to convince people that Smith was the man to vote for in the November election.

While Dutch agreed with his father's Democrat-leaning ways, he was too busy with his lifeguard duties at Lowell Park during the summer to do much active campaigning for Smith. Nonetheless, he did what he could, taking part in a demonstration march in town to protest bringing in outside workers to work on the farms and in the factories of Dixon. He also wore a "Vote for Smith" badge on his lifeguard suit. It wasn't much, but it was the best Dutch could do, given his busy schedule. Dutch found himself looking forward to the day when he would be old enough to vote and have his say in the political direction of the country.

Like all high school seniors, Dutch felt the future looming heavily over him. Almost everyone else in his graduating class expected to get a local job, marry, and raise a family in Dixon or one of the surrounding towns. No one spoke of leaving Illinois. Dutch, though, had a secret dream. After watching so many movies, he decided that he would like to be a Hollywood actor. This was not something he felt comfortable telling anyone about. He knew the whole notion sounded impossible.

The question for him became, what should he do that might help him achieve this goal? He knew that college was probably the next logical step for him. He had worked as hard as he could, taking on extra after-school jobs, but his savings amounted to only four hundred dollars. This was a lot of money for a high school boy to have saved, but not enough to pay for college. Margaret Cleaver was off to attend Eureka College, a Christian college about one hundred miles south of Dixon. Dutch decided that he wanted to join her and play football at Eureka College. But Margaret's parents were helping to pay for her education, while Dutch's parents could not afford to cover his.

As class president, Dutch gave a speech at graduation. During the speech he quoted John 10:10 from the Bible, "I came that they may have life, and have it abundantly." It was an inspiring speech, and as he sat down after giving it, Dutch knew that the time for words was over. Now that he had graduated from high school, somehow he had to find a way to make the abundant life that lay before him come to pass.

Chapter 5

Eureka College

On a hot September morning in 1928, Dutch Reagan helped Margaret Cleaver pile her suitcases into the rumble seat of her coupe. Margaret was off to college, and Dutch had decided to do everything he could to follow her. He had a plan. He'd already contacted Dean Harrod at Eureka College, and the dean had agreed to talk with Dutch about the possibility of enrollment and scholarships. Dean Harrod had also offered Dutch a night's stay at one of the fraternity houses on campus. Dutch leaped at the chance to meet with the dean and so decided to travel with Margaret to the college. He hoped that he would be able to make a good impression on Dean Harrod once he arrived.

Soon Dutch and Margaret were off, headed south from Dixon toward Eureka, Illinois. As they passed fields spread with crops of wheat and corn, Dutch prayed fervently that he would not be making the return trip home to Dixon the next day aboard a Greyhound bus.

Dutch and Margaret made good progress covering the hundred miles between Dixon and Eureka College, and by late afternoon Dutch was ready for the biggest interview of his life so far. Dean Harrod was a solid man who wore glasses and had a firm handshake. After he had welcomed Dutch to the college campus, Dutch dived right into his pitch. He presented the dean with the idea that Eureka College should extend to him a football scholarship. Much to Dutch's relief, Dean Harrod seemed open to the idea and sent Dutch to talk with the football coach, Ralph McKinzie.

Dutch took a deep breath as he walked into the football coach's office. He sensed that this would be his only chance to convince the coach that he was worthy of a football scholarship. The only problem was Dutch had never been the star of his high school football team. Still, Dutch did his best to sound like he would be an important addition to Eureka College's Golden Tornadoes football team.

Somehow Dutch did such a good job of convincing Coach McKinzie that he was offered a sports scholarship that would cover half his tuition for the year. Dean Harrod also offered Dutch a job washing dishes at the Tau Kappa Epsilon fraternity house, or TEKE, as everyone referred to it, in exchange for free meals. On top of this, Dutch would owe $270 for his room for the year, plus a $5 enrollment fee. Dutch did the math quickly in his head. He had $400 in the bank, and he would have to spend $90 for half his tuition cost, plus $275 in room and enrollment fees. That would leave him with the grand sum of $35 to survive on for a year. Could he do it? If it meant going to college and being near Margaret Cleaver, Dutch decided that of course he could.

Dutch enrolled in Eureka College on the spot and sent word to his mother in Dixon to bundle up his clothes and send them to him. Nelle Reagan's son was now a college student.

Dutch's good fortune continued. He was allocated a single room in the attic of the TEKE House. The room suited him fine. It had a dormer window from which he could see right across the tree-lined college campus.

Life at Eureka College turned out to be even more fun than Dutch had imagined it would be. He was away from his home and family for the first time, and he had a room to himself. So many opportunities were around campus that he scarcely knew which ones to choose, so he chose most of them!

Dutch's official academic subjects were French, history, English literature, math, physical education, and rhetoric. He liked to joke that he didn't let these stand in the way of his education. He made sure that he got passing grades in all his subjects so that he could pursue the extracurricular activities he really loved, such as football, swimming, and drama.

The college campus was relatively small, and only 220 students were enrolled, with most of them coming from poor, rural backgrounds similar to Dutch's. Eureka College itself was also poor, since tuition fees alone did not fully cover the cost of running the place. Everyone scrimped and saved where he could. Professors sometimes went for months without being paid their salaries, and the students helped run a co-op farm on the property. There was never much money left over for the college or the students, but somehow they got by. Dutch was glad that he had not attended one of the bigger state colleges, where a large number of students were from wealthy backgrounds. How much harder it would have been for him to have to worry about the clothes he wore or the fact that he did not own a car.

Dutch did not do so well at football, or at least not as well as he had portrayed he could. Coach McKinzie soon realized that Dutch was very nearsighted and so sat him on the bench for most games. Undeterred, Dutch plodded on, never missing a practice. However, Dutch's natural abilities in swimming were quickly appreciated. Dutch quickly learned how to do tumble turns and how to pace himself swimming laps in the still water of the pool. Within weeks he was representing the school at swim meets, where he always swam strongly and won many of his races.

Dutch and Margaret joined the Dramatic Club together, with Dutch dreaming of landing the leading roles. Within a month or two, Dutch was having so much fun that life back in Dixon seemed more like a thousand miles away than a hundred.

In late October, Ruth and Ed Graybill, his employers at Lowell Park, visited Dutch. They wanted to make sure that he would be coming back to Dixon to work as a lifeguard at the park during the summer of 1929. They also brought bad news. Moon had lost his job with the cement company and now worked at another job for much less money. And worse, the Fashion Boot Shop was in danger of closing and leaving his father without a job. Dutch was too far away to do much to help the situation, but it made him even more determined to stay in college. Dropping out now and taking a low-paying job might help out in the short term, but Dutch was convinced that in the long run he would be able to help his family more if he stayed and earned a college degree.

As Thanksgiving 1928 approached, Eureka College had descended into turmoil. Since tuition did not fully cover the cost of running the school, the balance was usually made up by grants, donations, and other aid given by various Disciples of Christ churches, the denomination with which Eureka College was loosely affiliated. But grants and giving were down, which led to inevitable finger-pointing. And many of those fingers were pointed at the college's president, Bert Wilson. In response to dwindling funds, President Wilson had attempted to make the college more appealing to church donors by cutting out even the mildest activities that might look "ungodly" to the outside world.

It was the 1920s, and flappers were dancing up a storm around the country. More liberal and tolerant attitudes were taking root regarding the place of women in contemporary society and a number of other social issues. These changes were shaking up things at other colleges across the nation, but not at Eureka College, which was out of step with city colleges. Girls still had to wear their skirts to midcalf with thick, not sheer, stockings, while boys had to wear shirts and ties to class. This year President Wilson had even stopped an old school tradition called "The Grind." This event had been the traditional way the first-year students met each other. The orchestra played while concentric circles of male and female students moved slowly in opposite directions from each other. As he passed a female student, each male student would reach out and shake her hand and introduce himself. In this way all the new students were introduced to each other, after which everyone sat down for ice cream while the faculty gave speeches. But Dutch's class had been denied this tradition, as it was deemed by President Wilson to provide too much physical contact.

A large portion of the student body chafed at such restrictions. Students wanted to dance and kick up their heels once in a while, and so they were forced to sneak into town, especially on Saturday nights, to find the fun they were looking for. Things reached a peak in November. Already the president had closed down the college's art and home economics programs, and when news came that the sports program would be next, the students decided that they'd had enough of Bert Wilson and his restrictions.

In a united voice, the student body called for President Wilson's resignation, which he finally tendered. However, the board of trustees of the college then had to choose to accept or reject his resignation.

It seemed that the trustees were happy with the new direction in which President Wilson had been taking the school, because they voted not to accept his resignation.

The student body, along with many faculty members, were incensed when they heard the news. None were more incensed than the members of the TEKE House. Two members of the fraternity had been leading the campaign to be rid of President Wilson, and now that the board of trustees had spurned their effort, their frustration boiled over. It was time for more action!

At 11:45 PM on the night of November 27, 1928, the college bell began to clang. It rang for fifteen minutes, and as it rang, students, faculty, and townspeople poured out into the chilly night air and headed for the center of the college campus. Dutch supposed that most of them thought there was a fire at the college, but the people soon found out differently. Members of the TEKE House had rung the bell to call people to an impromptu meeting. Soon the college chapel was packed to capacity with pajama-clad people.

The meeting had been called to protest the board of trustees' decision not to accept President Wilson's resignation and to call for a boycott of classes when the students returned from Thanksgiving break—a boycott that the students hoped would lead to the president's ouster from the school.

The leaders of the push to get rid of President Wilson decided that a freshman should be the one to lay out their complaint against the college president

and call for the boycott. They came to this conclusion because they believed that freshmen were the
ones who would be affected the most by the president's new rules and initiatives, since they still had
three years to go at Eureka College to earn their
degrees. The freshman that the members of TEKE
House chose to deliver their message was Dutch
Reagan. The leaders quickly schooled Dutch in all
he needed to cover in the course of his speech and
the action that they wanted the students to take.
Dutch listened carefully to what they told him, and
then it was time for him to speak.

Dutch stood and faced the gathered crowd. He
was amazed at how big it was. Every seat in the
chapel was full, people stood packed together in the
aisles and the doorways, and still others peered in
the windows from outside to see what was going on.
The room fell silent as Dutch opened his mouth and
began to speak. He laid out for the audience the
negotiations that had already gone on in relation to
forcing President Wilson's resignation from the college and the betrayal of the board of trustees in not
bowing to the will of the student body and accepting
the resignation.

As he spoke, Dutch was amazed at the rapport
that quickly developed between him and the audience. Even though he had acted in many plays
before, this was something different. This time he felt
that he had power over the audience; the students
were with him, and he could lead them wherever he
wanted them to go. The place he wanted them to
go was a boycott of classes upon their return from

Thanksgiving break. As he laid out the planned boycott, the crowd rose to their feet and cheered to signal their support. Even faculty members and townspeople were on their feet. A statement declaring the students' intent to boycott was quickly drawn up and signed, and by 2:00 AM the meeting was over.

Dutch returned home for Thanksgiving break, still reeling from the exhilaration he had felt in front of the crowd. He had been in control; he felt he could have persuaded that crowd to do almost anything he wanted them to do.

Back home in Dixon, things were as bad as Ruth and Ed Graybill had said they were. Yet through it all, Nelle remained her positive self. Dutch was glad when Thanksgiving break was over and it was time to head back to Eureka College. He was eager to see how the boycott would play out and whether the students would get their way.

On the first day back at college, Dutch and the other members of TEKE House were gratified when only six students, two of whom were President Wilson's daughters, showed up for class. For the next week no more students broke solidarity and began attending classes. The student revolt at Eureka College was soon big news. United Press covered the incident, and their reports were printed in many large newspapers, including *The New York Times* and the *Chicago Tribune.*

The impasse at Eureka College was broken on December 7, when Bert Wilson resigned as president of the college and announced to the board of trustees that his resignation was irrevocable this time. The student body had won the day, and Dutch Reagan had played a hand in it.

Dutch continued to enjoy his extracurricular activities that year, though he struggled to prove to Coach McKinzie that he should be in the football starting lineup. When the school year was over, summer was much the same as other summers. Dutch returned to Dixon and went back to work as a lifeguard at Lowell Park. In quiet moments he loved to take Margaret rowing on the Rock River in the park rowboat.

Money was tougher than ever, however. Dutch's parents lived in the same one-bedroom house, and his brother Moon had grown depressed with his low-paying job. To make matters worse, by the end of the summer, Dutch had saved only two hundred dollars, not enough to pay for another year at Eureka College.

Dutch was concerned about what to do next. He wanted to continue his college education but realized he could not afford the tuition cost at that time. Then a land surveyor he had met at Lowell Park over the summer came up with a solution. He offered Dutch a deal. If Dutch would work for the man as his rodman for a year, the surveyor would help him to get a rowing scholarship at the University of Wisconsin the following year.

Stuck as to what to do next, Dutch accepted the deal and made plans to show up to work for the surveyor instead of returning to Eureka College. He probably would have done just that, except for one thing.

Chapter 6

Depression Days

Rain. Dutch lay on his cot in the living room and listened. Yes, there was no doubt about it—it was raining, hard. Dutch got up and parted the blinds. The ground was already muddy, and a gray sky hung low. It had apparently been raining most of the night, and it seemed as though it would continue on through the rest of the day.

Dutch sighed as he dressed. There was no use showing up for his new surveying job on a day like today. It was much too wet and muddy for surveying.

As Dutch finished buttoning his shirt, the telephone rang. He picked it up.

"Hi," came the voice of Margaret Cleaver over the line. "I just called to ask what you were going to do today. Wouldn't you like to drive back to Eureka

with me and see everyone? You could take the Greyhound bus back tonight."

Since Dutch had nothing else to do, he agreed to
the plan. Soon he and Margaret were chatting away
as Margaret drove her coupe southward through the
rain. Mostly they talked about Margaret's upcoming
classes. As they talked, Dutch could not help but
think of the high hopes he'd had a year earlier. Now
he was a college dropout, though he didn't like to
think of it in those terms, and the notion did not sit
well with him.

Margaret pulled her car to a halt at Eureka College. Once Dutch had climbed out and again set foot
on college property, he was sure that he could not
leave. What had he been thinking? Soon a number
of the returning students were shaking his hand and
welcoming him back on campus. They did not know
that Dutch was only visiting, and they, too, started
talking about all the exciting things that were going
to happen that year.

Before he knew it, Dutch was back in Dean Harrod's office figuring out how he could stay at Eureka
College for the 1929–1930 school year. Half an hour
later, Dutch had a job washing dishes in the women's
dormitory and a needy student scholarship, which
meant that the college would let him pay half his
tuition for the year upfront and pay the other half
after he graduated. Elated, Dutch called his mother
to tell her to send his trunk of clothes to Eureka College as soon as possible.

Dutch was even assigned to the same room he'd
had the year before. Happily, he once again peered

out the dormer window in the attic across campus. Only one thing could have made the experience even better—having his brother Moon there with him.

This seemed an odd thing for Dutch to think. Dutch and Moon had never been particularly close and had taken different directions in life. Dutch realized that Moon was probably way too worldly for a small Christian college, but he knew it bothered his mother that Moon had not gone on to college. Over the summer his mother had put pressure on Dutch to help his brother find a way to get to college. But as far as Dutch could see, that was not the biggest problem. The biggest problem was that Moon, who was three years older than Dutch, did not *want* to go to college. Nonetheless, in deference to his mother's wishes, Dutch sought out Coach McKinzie. If a way had been found for Dutch to attend Eureka College for another year, maybe a way could be found for Moon to attend also.

Much to Dutch's surprise, the coach listened carefully as Dutch described his older brother's prowess on the football field. Moon had played tight end the year Dixon High School won the county high school football championship. Coach McKinzie was impressed and offered Moon a partial athletic scholarship. This was a start.

Next, Dutch went back to see whether Dean Harrod would allow Moon to defer half of his tuition until after graduation and whether a campus job was available for him. The answer was yes to both questions. All Moon had to do was come up with an additional ten dollars a month and he could attend college. Dutch called his mother and relayed the good news to her, though he was sure that Moon would turn down the opportunity. Still, Dutch told himself, that was not *his* problem. He had done his best.

The following afternoon Moon Reagan arrived at Eureka College with two trunks, his own and his brother's. Sheepishly he told Dutch the story of how he came to be there. The night before, their mother had told him about the opportunity to attend Eureka College. As Dutch expected, Moon had simply laughed the whole thing off. He was still laughing about the idea of his going to college the next morning when he showed up for work. When his boss, Mr. Kennedy, asked Moon what was so funny, Moon told him about the offer to go to college and his mother's crazy aspirations for him, which he was going to have no part of. At ten o'clock that same morning, the secretary came to Moon and said, "Here's your paycheck, Mr. Reagan."

Moon was puzzled. It was not Friday, his usual payday. "My paycheck?" he said. "It's not payday."

"It is for you!" the secretary replied.

"Am I fired?" Moon asked.

"Call it whatever you like," the secretary said. "Mr. Kennedy says that if you are not smart enough to take advantage of the good thing your brother did for you in fixing you up to go to college, you're not smart enough to work here."

Moon was dumbfounded, but he could see that the secretary was serious. He cleared out his locker and headed for home. Along the way he decided that he might as well go to Eureka. It would be better than sitting around his parents' house waiting for a job.

Dutch laughed when Moon told him the story. He could just hear his mother saying, "God works in mysterious ways!" And apparently He had.

Moon was a far better football player than Dutch, and the natural rivalry between the two brothers continued on the football field. Football was about the only area the two had in common; Moon was not interested in swimming or acting.

On October 29, 1929, the New York Stock Exchange suffered a major crash in the value of shares traded on the exchange. This drop in value destroyed some people financially. Dutch read with interest about the crash in the local newspaper, but the events far away in New York had little impact on him or those living in Eureka or the other small communities of rural Illinois. The economic good times that had swept the country during the 1920s did not seem to make it as far as places like Eureka, Dixon, Tampico, and any number of other rural towns.

The school year passed swiftly. Dutch studied just enough to slip by, while Margaret won the highest grades in the class. Margaret and Dutch appeared together in *Aria da Capo* at a national drama contest at Northwestern University in Evanston, Illinois, where they placed third.

Dutch continued to read in the newspaper about the deepening depression that now gripped the country as a result of the stock market crash. Breadlines were become commonplace in a number of cities as out-of-work men struggled to feed their families.

Compared to those grappling with such circumstances, Dutch decided that he was in a good place, but he was concerned about what the worsening economic conditions would mean for his parents.

Dutch, Moon, and Margaret all returned to Dixon for the summer of 1930. All three of them were determined to finish their degree programs, though Margaret was considering transferring to a state university where she would have more academic opportunities. Dutch tried to talk her out of such a move, but her conviction that she should attend the University of Illinois in Champaign grew stronger as the summer progressed.

As fall approached, it was decided. For the first time since they had started dating five summers before, Dutch and Margaret would go their separate ways. Dutch tried to put on a brave face. Once back at Eureka College, he threw himself into his junior year. He won a varsity letter in swimming and became the coach as well as the star of the swimming team. He also was an editor of the yearbook, was treasurer of his fraternity, and played the lead in four dramatic productions. It sounded like a lot of work, until Dutch reminded himself what a small college Eureka was and how everyone had to wear more than one hat.

Once again the year sped by. The Reagan brothers headed back for the summer to Dixon, where Dutch looked forward to being reacquainted with Margaret. For the sixth year, he worked as a lifeguard at Lowell Park. Dutch felt luckier than ever to have a job. Everywhere he looked in Dixon he saw the effects of the Great Depression. The factories that employed many of the men in town were closing down one by one, and farmers, unable to pay their mortgages, were walking off their land. Dutch had never imagined he would see such a sight, and he knew that he would never forget it.

The Fashion Boot Shop finally went under financially, and Jack Reagan found a lower-paying job as a traveling shoe salesman. Meanwhile, Nelle took a job as a salesclerk and seamstress at a women's-wear shop, where she worked long hours for fourteen dollars a week.

The only piece of good news, as far as Dutch was concerned, was that Margaret was returning to Eureka College for her senior year. Even this good news was tainted by the fact that her father had transferred from Dixon to be the new pastor in Eureka, which meant that Margaret would no longer be living on campus but would be living at home with her parents to save money. Still, Dutch was happy that he and Margaret would be together again.

A similar scholarship package to that of the previous two years was worked out for the Reagan brothers. Dutch went back to Eureka College for his senior year, and Moon entered his junior year. Dutch was elected senior class president and made his way to a respectable spot on the football team. He still dreamed of a professional career in the sport, though when he really thought about it, he knew it was not going to happen.

Dutch and Moon returned to Dixon for Christmas 1931, just in time for Jack Reagan to announce that he had been fired. There was not much to celebrate. Nelle rented out the bedroom of their one-bedroom house, and the four members of the Reagan family huddled together in the living room. They used a small electric hotplate to cook on, and Dutch worried about how his parents were going to cope as the year went on.

When Dutch got back to college, his mother wrote to say that she and Jack were struggling to the point where neighbors were bringing them plates of food. The news saddened Dutch, who was used to his mother being the one doling out charity, not the one receiving it. In response, Dutch scraped together fifty dollars that he had planned to use to get himself through the rest of the school year and sent it off to his mother.

Dutch began to feel the effects of the depression at college. Although he was on the yearbook team, no money was available to produce a yearbook, and the Golden Tornadoes football team could no longer afford to travel off campus. The team played only home games. Students, too, feeling pressure from home, began to drop out one by one. By the time of graduation, only forty-five students remained in the senior class. Dutch was proud to be one of them.

As senior class president, Dutch made a speech to the crowd that gathered for the graduation ceremony. Margaret won the award for the highest grades in the school, and the Reverend Cleaver prayed for them all and blessed them.

The graduation ceremony ended with a tradition peculiar to Eureka College. No one was sure how it started, but all of the graduating students stood in a circle holding onto a length of rope woven from ivy that had been cut from the vines that grew up the brick dormitory walls. Each student took a turn breaking off the piece of rope he or she held, signifying that the student was breaking with the old life and moving on to a new one. There was only one exception: any couple who wanted to declare they were going on from college together as a couple held onto the rope between them and did not break it.

Dutch Reagan stood next to Margaret Cleaver during the ivy ceremony. When it came their time to break the vine, they looked into each other's eyes and held fast. Dutch was proud. They were a couple, facing the future together, whatever that future might hold.

Chapter 7

On the Radio

Thankfully, Dutch was able to return to his summer job as a lifeguard at Lowell Park, though he knew the job would come to a natural end at the conclusion of summer. He was one of the few men in Dixon with a steady job. Things were bleaker than ever at home and in the community. Farmers continued to walk off their farms, leaving their dairy herds behind. The price of milk had dropped so much that it was no longer worth milking the cows.

Churches begged for donations of fruit and vegetables and then enlisted the help of experts from the University of Illinois Agriculture Department who brought ten large pressure cookers to town. Women from all nineteen of Dixon's churches banded together and produced 5,891 cans of food for the hungriest citizens of the town.

Dutch was happy to be able to provide a safe environment at Lowell Park, where the children of Dixon could go and forget their problems for an afternoon. He also hoped that the park would hold the key to his future. Over the seven summers he'd worked there, he had come to know many wealthy families who spent part of their vacation in or around Dixon. Dutch hoped that he would be able to use one of these connections to land a job.

One summer afternoon, Dutch found himself sitting next to Sid Altschuler, a successful businessman from Kansas City. "What do you plan to do when summer is over?" Sid asked Dutch.

Dutch thought for a moment, wishing that he had something impressive to say. After all, he'd just graduated from college with a degree in economics, but nothing came to mind. "I don't know," he answered.

"Well," Sid replied, "I'll give you a few days to think about it, and when you decide, I'll do what I can to get your foot in the door. I have a lot of connections."

Dutch nodded in gratitude. He knew Sid would be a great advocate, if only he could make up his mind about what he wanted to do. The more Dutch thought about it, the more conflicted he became. How absurd it was to be thinking about what he wanted to do when so many other able-bodied men would take any job offered to them. Dutch chastised himself for being selfish during such a bad recession, but he couldn't help himself. He looked at the forty years of work ahead of him and wanted to choose something that he was passionate about and that would make him want to show up for work every day. But what was it?

Dutch tried to settle on one thing he wanted to do, but he had three interests that he loved—interests that could keep him up all night thinking and strategizing. They were sports, acting, and—since his involvement in the student revolt during his first year at Eureka College—politics. He could not decide which of the three he liked the best. Sometimes he was drawn to one, and sometimes another. All of this did not make choosing a career path easy.

Of his three interests, Dutch decided that acting was the most improbable one to follow. But he struck on an idea: if acting was improbable, what about being on the radio? From the first time Dutch had heard the primitive crystal set radio at his relatives' farm when he was a boy, he had been interested in radio. And in the intervening years, radio had come a long way. By now most homes had a radio, which was no longer of the crystal set variety that you needed to use headphones to listen to. Instead, radios were now polished wooden cabinets containing rows of valves and the latest electronics and had large speakers that could fill a room with sound. And Chicago was the hub for radio throughout the entire Midwest. Surely he could land a job on the radio! Jubilantly, Dutch told Sid that he was interested in becoming a radio announcer. Unfortunately, Sid said that radio was the one field where he had no contacts at all. Dutch was disappointed that Sid could not help him, but not too disappointed. After all, now he knew what he wanted to do.

From that day on, Dutch practiced the skills of his new profession at every opportunity. No child who came near him at Lowell Park left without a thirty-second sound bite of some imagined football commentary. Soon all the regulars at the park knew that Dutch wanted to become a radio announcer.

At the end of summer, his lifeguard duties over, Dutch set his plans into motion. He hitchhiked from Dixon to Eureka to see Margaret and then moved on to Chicago. He had a college friend in Chicago with whom he could stay for a few nights. Dutch's plan was to land an interview with someone at NBC and talk the person into hiring him as a sportscaster.

Things did not go well, however. This was the first time Dutch had been to Chicago on his own, and he had to admit that the place scared him. The buses looked huge and menacing as they lurched around corners and screeched to a halt. Some of the buildings were twenty stories high and trapped the sweltering heat down at street level. And everyone seemed to be going somewhere in a hurry. Dutch was used to small, friendly towns and found it hard to even get someone to stop long enough so that he could ask for directions. Finally, he made it to the downtown offices of NBC, only to be told that the program director conducted interviews only on Thursdays, and today was Tuesday.

The next day Dutch made his way to the Wrigley Building, where CBS had its offices. The reception-ist politely told him it would be impossible to get an interview with anyone in the company. Dutch moved on to the smaller radio stations in town. Everywhere he went, he heard the same story over and over again. No, they were not hiring, and even if they were, they had a list of qualified applicants that they would draw from.

What did a young man with an economics degree and work background as a lifeguard have to offer? That was a good question, but Dutch decided to ignore it. And the more he walked the streets of Chicago, the more convinced he became that he needed to be not just an announcer but a sports announcer.

Thursday came, and Dutch eagerly arrived at the NBC office. Perhaps this would be his big break. Alas, the receptionist informed him that the program director was not seeing anyone that day. Dutch stood for a moment, unwilling to leave the building. This had been his last hope.

The receptionist looked at him with pity in her eyes. "You know," she said, "you might be going about this the wrong way. You don't have the experience to get noticed in a big city like Chicago. Program directors are looking for people who are already well known, which you aren't."

Dutch nodded. After two days of beating the pavement, he had to agree with her assessment.

"But," the secretary added brightly, "you might have a shot at some tiny radio station in the middle of nowhere. It would be a chance to get your foot in the door, to learn the ropes. Why don't you find somewhere to get some experience and then come back in a year or so?"

Dutch mumbled his thanks. He did not really want to start in some two-bit announcing job. He could already see himself in the big time, but he had to face the truth. The receptionist was right: he wasn't going to be hired in Chicago anytime soon.

The ride back home to Dixon was depressing. Once again Dutch hitchhiked, and the rides he got were short. One driver who picked him up had just been skunk trapping, and the cab of the truck reeked with the pungent odor of skunk, which did not help Dutch's mood at all.

When Dutch got home, he told his parents about his experience. They tried to encourage him not to give up. Jack Reagan even offered to put ten dollars' worth of gas in the car so that Dutch could drive around to the towns in the area that had their own local radio stations. Dutch knew this was a huge sacrifice. He could not remember the last time anyone had gassed up the car and driven it.

That night, Dutch lay in bed and plotted his course for the following Monday. He would drive southwest to Davenport, Iowa, seventy-five miles away. Then he would head south toward Galesburg, loop around to the east, and then head back to Dixon.

On Monday, the weather was clear and not too cold. Dutch took that as a good sign as he set off in the car for Davenport. He covered the distance in record time. Because the Great Depression had thinned out the number of cars on the road, there was virtually no traffic to worry about on the drive.

When Dutch got to Davenport, it didn't take him long to find the local radio station, WOC. He parked the car, took a deep breath, straightened his tie, and stepped out. He had only one chance to make a big impression on this small town, and he knew it.

WOC was located on the top floor of the Palmer School of Chiropractic Medicine Building in downtown Davenport. After riding the elevator to the top floor, Dutch met the radio station's manager and top announcer, Peter MacArthur.

"I'm Dutch Reagan," he introduced himself before going on to explain why he was there.

Peter MacArthur, a Scotsman who spoke with a strong brogue and whose arthritis was so bad that he had to balance on two walking sticks to stand or move around, looked at Dutch for a moment. Dutch waited eagerly for the station manager's reply. Was this going to be his big break? Alas, it wasn't. Peter explained that he had just hired a new announcer for the radio station.

Disappointment and frustration descended over Dutch like a cloud. "How does anyone get a chance as a sports announcer if you can't get a job in a radio station?" he asked.

With that, Dutch turned, left the radio station, and headed down the corridor to the elevator. He was so caught up in his thoughts and feelings that he failed to hear the station manager calling after him. As he waited for the elevator to arrive, Dutch suddenly became aware of a cane rapping him on the shin. He spun around, and there stood Peter.

"Not so fast," the manager said. "Didn't ye hear me calling ye?"

Dutch shook his head.

"Well, do ye perhaps know football?" Peter inquired.

As quickly as he could, Dutch told him about playing football in both high school and college, making his contribution to the teams seem bigger than it really was. Before he knew it, Dutch was in the studio, ready to demonstrate his football announcing skills. He sat for a moment in the blue velvet–lined studio and recalled the football game the previous fall between Eureka College and Western State University.

When the red light in the studio flicked on, Dutch leaned close to the microphone and began a commentary on the fourth quarter of that game. "We're going into the fourth quarter now. A chill wind is blowing in through the end of the stadium," he began. And just as he had been doing all summer long for people at Lowell Park, Dutch launched into a play-by-play account of the game, making up any details he had forgotten as he went along.

Twenty minutes later, Peter MacArthur burst through the studio door. "Ye did great!" he exclaimed.

Although Peter didn't offer Dutch a permanent job at the radio station, he did offer him the chance to prove himself some more as a sports announcer. He would pay Dutch five dollars and cover his bus fare if he would travel to Iowa City the following Saturday to help announce the college football game being played there. Although it wasn't completely what he had hoped for, Dutch jumped at the opportunity.

The next Saturday afternoon Dutch found himself sitting in the broadcast booth in Iowa City. A more experienced announcer was to cover most of the game, and Dutch's job was to add color and description and offer commentary between plays and quarters. Dutch relished the opportunity and gave his best at every chance he had to speak into the microphone.

To Dutch's and his fellow announcer's surprise, before the start of the fourth quarter, Peter sent a note up to the broadcast booth that simply read, "Let the kid finish the game." And that is what Dutch did.

After the football broadcast, Peter offered Dutch the opportunity to announce three more football games from Iowa City.

Dutch spent hours at home reading everything he could about the football teams who were going to be playing. He had a great memory, which helped him out many times. When there was a lapse in the play on the field, he inserted some interesting facts he had learned about the teams and their various players.

Even though he studied up on the teams whose games he was going to announce, Dutch still had plenty of time to spare, and he spent a lot of it studying and discussing politics. The 1932 presidential election was fast approaching. The country was in the depths of economic despair. To make matters worse, as president, Herbert Hoover had done little to alleviate the suffering and hardship that had engulfed the lives of so many Americans. Dutch read with interest newspaper accounts of the reaction to Hoover as he campaigned to be reelected president. On one occasion at a campaign stop in Detroit, the crowd had begun chanting, "Hang Hoover! Hang Hoover!" And at other stops people had shaken their fists at the president and pelted his limousine with eggs and tomatoes.

Like his father, Dutch was a strong Democrat, and the Democratic candidate for president that year,

Franklin Delano Roosevelt, inspired him. Roosevelt seemed to understand the nature of the problem that the country had fallen into, and he promised immediate action if he was elected. He would use the power of the government to create jobs, get people back to work, and stop the flow of farmers forced to walk off their land.

Roosevelt's approach to the problem made a lot of sense to Dutch, and at the age of twenty-one, Dutch cast his first vote ever for the Democrat. To Dutch's delight, Roosevelt won the presidential election in a landslide, carrying forty-two of the forty-eight states.

Meanwhile, Dutch was settling into his new role as a sports announcer. He felt confident and in control, and it showed in the broadcast booth. The critic from the *Chicago Tribune* noticed, too, and wrote in the paper, "[Dutch Reagan's] crisp account of the muddy struggle sounded like a carefully written story of the gridiron goings-on, and his quick tongue seemed to be as fast as the plays."

Christmas 1932 brought Dutch one of the best Christmas presents ever—the offer of a permanent, full-time job as a staff announcer at WOC. The job came with a starting salary of one hundred dollars a month. This seemed like a fortune to Dutch, who had no doubt in his mind about accepting the job.

Early in the new year, Dutch moved into a rented room in Davenport, Iowa. The room cost him $8 a week, and he bought a meal ticket at the Palmer School of Chiropractic Medicine's cafeteria for another $3.65. He also sent $5 to his mother to help out at home and $2.50 to his brother Moon to help cover costs during his last semester at Eureka College. (Dutch had asked the local Christian Church pastor for permission to use his tithe to help out his brother rather than giving it to the church. The pastor agreed that God would bless such use of the money.) This left Dutch with a little over $5 a week, some of which went to paying off his student loan. The money may not have gone as far as Dutch would have liked, but it did accomplish the things that were most important to him—helping his family through hard times and paying back his debt.

Still, Dutch did one thing every morning that made him feel like he earned a million dollars. On the way to work at the radio station, he gave a dime to the first man who asked for money to buy a cup of coffee. Doing this always put a smile on Dutch's face as he entered the studio.

Surprisingly, the day-to-day work of being a radio announcer was not as glamorous as Dutch had imagined it to be. But, he told himself, it was a job at a time when jobs were becoming scarcer by the day.

Like so many people, Dutch waited anxiously for Franklin Delano Roosevelt to be sworn into office on March 4, 1933. Everyone hoped that things in the country would then begin to change. Dutch listened with interest when, on March 12, eight days after being sworn in, Roosevelt took to the radio to have what he called a "Fireside Chat" with the American people. Roosevelt reassured the population that the banks were safe and that it was better for people to keep what cash they had in the bank rather than under the mattress at home. Dutch was as amazed as anyone to learn that by the end of the next day people had poured into the banks to deposit their money, so much so that deposits far outweighed withdrawals.

In late April 1933, Peter MacArthur called Dutch into his office. Big changes were afoot. WOC and another radio station from Des Moines, Radio WHO, were joining forces. Peter told Dutch that he wanted him to transfer to Des Moines, where he would be made the chief sports announcer with a salary of two hundred dollars a month, twice his current salary. Dutch did not hesitate for a second in agreeing to the move. It was the best news he'd had in weeks.

Dutch hurried off to telephone his mother and tell her about the new job. His mother was delighted. After he had talked to his mother, Dutch called Margaret Cleaver, who was teaching in a small town nearby.

"Well," she countered, after Dutch told her his news. "I have some news of my own. My sister Helen and I are planning to move to France for a year."

"When?" Dutch asked lamely.

"In June."

"Where does that leave us?" Dutch inquired.

"With time to ourselves," came Margaret's flat reply.

Dutch hung up the telephone, feeling like a deflated man. Did this mean that his seven-year relationship with Margaret was over? He wasn't sure, but it certainly sounded like it.

As a result, Dutch was about to hit the airwaves of Des Moines as one of the city's most eligible bachelors.

A Household Name

Compared to Davenport, Des Moines felt like the big time. The city had a population of 142,000, all of whom, it seemed to Dutch, loved listening to the radio. In early 1933, just before Dutch moved to Des Moines, radio station WHO had updated its broadcast signal power to fifty thousand watts, allowing listeners throughout a large portion of the Midwest to clearly tune in the station. The station was quickly developing innovative radio programs to appeal to its large audience. These new programs offered advice on everything from raising a calf to finding a job.

Dutch loved being in the middle of the hustle and bustle of a growing medium like radio, and soon he was not only the station's chief sports announcer but also the announcer on the H. R. Gross newscast.

The sponsor of the newscast was Kentucky Club, a pipe-tobacco company. In keeping with his new role, Dutch started to smoke a pipe.

Dutch was a charming figure around town, and no more so than when he entered Cy's Moonlight Club, the swankiest club in Des Moines. The place got its reputation from being the only club in town with a jukebox where people could dance the night away while listening to music played on the jukebox. Although Dutch never drank much alcohol, he enjoyed meeting his coworkers at Cy's for an evening of socializing. Even though Prohibition was still in force, the owner of the club openly sold near beer spiked with alcohol, the same concoction Dutch's father had turned to at the start of Prohibition. To Dutch's surprise, despite selling alcohol, Cy's Moonlight Club never seemed to be raided by the police for violating the law.

Sometimes Dutch would date one of the women at the radio station, but in his heart he was never sure whether he and Margaret had broken up or just taken a break from each other. Dutch hoped that Margaret would return to Eureka after her time in France and that the two of them would pick up their relationship where it had left off. Much to Dutch's chagrin, this was not to be.

Three months after Dutch arrived in Des Moines, Margaret wrote to tell him that she was engaged to a young American man she had met in Paris. Dutch was devastated by the news. Soon afterward, his mother called with more bad news. Jack Reagan had suffered a serious heart attack. He had survived, but he was weak, and the doctor predicted that he would never work again.

The mainstay of the sports program at WHO was baseball, and part of Dutch's job was to broadcast Chicago Cubs games on the radio. However, Dutch was not actually present at the games he announced. Instead, he was tucked away in his small, ground-floor studio at the radio station in Des Moines. Dutch's magic was making it seem to his listeners that he was actually at the game. To do this, an ingenious system had been put into place. A telegraph operator sat in the press box at Chicago's Wrigley Field, the Cubs home field. He transmitted each play of the game in Morse code to the radio studio in Des Moines, where an assistant transcribed the Morse code into a shorthand on sheets of paper. The sheets of paper were passed through the studio window to Dutch, perched behind the microphone. Dutch then deciphered the shorthand and announced the plays as if he were actually watching the game. To make things seem even more realistic, Dutch had a turntable that played a phonograph record of crowd applause. He operated the volume of the turntable by foot pedal. If, for example, a player hit a home run, Dutch would press down on the pedal to raise the volume of crowd noise, as if everyone in the bleachers around him was cheering.

Dutch was able to make his broadcasts seem so real that many of his listeners did not even know that he wasn't at the ball game. After Dutch had traveled to Chicago to watch the Cubs play at Wrigley Field, his broadcasts from Des Moines became even more realistic. He now knew what the inside of Wrigley Field, having never been there before, actually looked like. He also closely watched the various Cubs players' mannerisms on the field and was able to add much more detail to his descriptions of the players.

This extra knowledge helped Dutch greatly during one broadcast. The Cubs were playing the St. Louis Cardinals. The game had just entered the ninth inning in a scoreless tie when suddenly the telegraph wire from Wrigley Field went dead. Dutch's assistant told him of the situation. Without batting an eye, Dutch leaned into the microphone and continued with his broadcast, making up plays as he went along.

"Dizzy Dean is winding up for his pitch. Augie Galan is at bat for the Cubs. Here comes the pitch. It's a ball, low and on the outside." On Dutch went, calling a series of foul balls, trying to use up time in the hope that the telegraph wire would come to life again. "Galan drives it foul. A red-headed kid has scrambled and managed to get himself a souvenir ball."

After six and a half minutes of silence, the telegraph wire burst back to life. Dutch breathed a sigh of relief as his assistant began handing him sheets of paper with the actual plays scribbled on them in shorthand. He was soon back in full swing broadcasting the rest of the game. Few of his listeners ever learned that the telegraph line had gone dead and that for over six minutes Dutch had simply made up plays to fill the time.

By the end of summer Dutch had saved enough money to buy his first car—a two-seater brown Nash convertible. He bought the car over the phone from a friend who was now a car dealer in Eureka. Dutch asked his brother Moon, who had graduated from college but had not yet found a job, to go to Eureka, pick up the car, and drive it to Des Moines. When Moon arrived in Des Moines with the Nash, Dutch immediately fell in love with the car. Together the two brothers took it for a test drive around town.

Jobs were still tough to find, and Moon decided to stay with Dutch for a while and look for a job in Des Moines. Few were to be found.

One Friday night, Moon was hanging around the radio studio while Dutch broadcast his regular sports commentary, which included predictions as to who would win that weekend's football games. As Dutch spoke into the microphone, Moon shook his head. Evidently he did not agree with his brother's predictions. On the spur of the moment, Dutch decided to pick up on this. He quickly introduced Moon to his audience and then pushed the microphone over to him. "So tell us, who do you think will win, and why?" he asked him.

Moon, who had studied Dutch behind the microphone for some time, started straight in on his own predictions as if he had rehearsed them for days. Dutch was sure that the audience would enjoy the banter between the two of them, and they did. Peter MacArthur took note of Moon's talent behind the microphone and offered Moon a thirty-dollar-a-week job on the radio in Davenport. Moon took the job, much to Dutch's delight. It meant that he could now stop subsidizing his brother's living costs and get his room in Des Moines back to himself. Now both the Reagan brothers were on the air, and Dutch was happy with the way things were working out.

One of his girlfriends, Mary Frances, was an avid horsewoman, and Dutch's next adventure involved horses. Dutch had always admired horses from afar. As a boy he had read every Western he could get his hands on and seen every Western movie as well. He had often imagined himself on a tall, white horse, clicking the reins, digging his heels into the stirrups, and galloping off into the sunset. Now he decided to figure out a way to make this a reality.

Money, however, was a barrier. Buying and keeping a horse was an expensive enterprise, and Dutch did not have that kind of money. Then one of his fellow announcers at WHO had an idea. The Fourteenth Cavalry Regiment was stationed at nearby Camp Dodge, and the War Department was accepting candidates into the Citizens Military Training Program for the reserve cavalry. The announcer suggested that Dutch apply.

At first Dutch laughed off the idea. His eyesight was too poor to pass the medical examination. But then he heard some great news—the cavalry did not conduct the medical examination until the recruit had passed all of his tests and other exams. Dutch found this hard to believe, but when he inquired, he was assured that it was true.

Dutch had found himself a way to learn to ride. He signed up for the once-a-week classes and the correspondence course to become an officer in the reserve cavalry. Now he was free to drive out to Camp Dodge anytime he wanted and train on the magnificent cavalry horses. The length of training time was open-ended, and Dutch figured he could "train" for several years before someone higher up forced him to take the final test and subsequent medical examination.

Dutch was proud of the new life he had made for himself in Des Moines. He quickly rose to be the most recognized person on the radio throughout the Midwest for Big Ten football and major league baseball. Chicago Cubs fans across the region knew his voice and trusted his broadcasts.

In time, Dutch Reagan became a household name. Everyone in Des Moines seemed to know who he was. Now that he was so well known, he could easily have moved on to work at a radio station in Chicago, as he had originally planned, but something held him back.

Dutch took frequent trips back to Dixon, Illinois, where his parents continued to struggle financially. He thought about moving them to Des Moines, where he could keep an eye on them, but somehow Des Moines did not feel like Dutch's permanent home. But where was his permanent home? The question eluded Dutch. He was a small-town boy who had done well for himself—better than almost anyone else he knew—but he wanted more.

In early 1935 Dutch engineered a way to get out of Des Moines toward the end of the long, snowy winter. The Chicago Cubs held their spring training

camp on Santa Catalina Island, just off the coast
of Long Beach, California. The Wrigley family, who
owned the Cubs, also owned the island. Dutch
approached the radio station manager with a deal.
If WHO was prepared to pay for a train ticket and
accommodations for him to join the Cubs during
spring training, he was prepared to use his vacation
time while he was there. Much to his amazement,
the deal was approved, and Dutch was soon packing
his clothes for a trip to California.

The train journey took two days—two wonderful
days during which Dutch sat glued to the window.
He had never been out West before, and watching
the scenery that flicked past was like looking at the
pages of a *National Geographic* magazine.

Dutch was in awe of the sheer size of the Rocky
Mountains and the barren vastness of the Mohave
Desert, which reminded him of the backdrop of a
hundred Western movies he had seen. And Los Angeles was the biggest and most sprawling city Dutch
had ever seen. But the size of Los Angeles did not
intimidate at all, because he was much more a man
of the world than he had been three years before
when he had gone to Chicago in search of a job on
the radio.

Dutch's stay on Catalina was magical. He got
to see how the rich and famous lived. Many of the
guests on the island sailed over on their own yachts
and dined at the island's small, exclusive restau-
rants. Dutch even got to see some movie sets that
had been left behind. The sets had been designed to
make Catalina island look like the South Pacific.

Then there was the time that Dutch spent with the Chicago Cubs. Training camp turned out to be a fairly relaxed time, and Dutch got to know and spend time with the players. He listened carefully to the stories they told him over drinks. The details would be great to fill in dead time on the airwaves later on.

When Dutch returned to Des Moines, the radio station manager agreed that the time at spring training camp had made Dutch's baseball commentaries more interesting. Dutch grinned. He knew that he would get to go back the next year. And sure enough, he returned to California for spring training in 1936 and again in 1937, though by the 1937 trip, he had something quite different in mind. In his private moments he sometimes admitted to himself that he still wanted to be an actor. And the only place to do that was in Hollywood, California, which he passed through on his way to Catalina. How much harder would it be to visit a few movie studios while he was in Hollywood?

In February 1937 Dutch took the usual train ride west, only this time when he arrived at Union Station in Los Angeles, he walked a few blocks in the pouring rain and checked into the Biltmore Hotel.

That night Dutch met up with a singer who had worked for WHO in Des Moines. Her name was Joy Hodges, and she had told Dutch to look her up in Los Angeles if he ever had the time. Now he had more than time—he had a plan.

Dutch asked Joy if she would introduce him to an agent who could tell him whether he had any talent at all, so that he would know whether to forget about being an actor or to pursue his dream.

Joy looked at him and then said, "Take off your glasses."

Dutch obediently did as she told him.

"Get rid of those glasses, and I'll take you in to see my agent tomorrow."

Dutch hardly slept that night. He was too excited—and a little nervous. He took Joy's advice seriously, but he wondered how he was going to make it through a meeting without his glasses. He just hoped that he did not trip on the way in.

At ten o'clock the next morning, Dutch found himself in the office of Bill Meiklejohn. It was hard for him to say what Bill, who was just a blur to Dutch, actually looked like. Nonetheless, Dutch listened carefully to make up for not being able to see much. He laid out for Bill his acting experience, which even Dutch had to admit sounded fairly insignificant. He also told Bill about what he was doing in radio in Des Moines. When he had finished, Bill picked up the telephone and called Max Arnow, the casting director for Warner Brothers Studio.

Dutch could hardly believe what he was hearing. "Max," Bill said into the phone. "I have another Robert Taylor sitting in my office." Robert Taylor was a star!

Still, the road ahead was not certain. Bill arranged for Dutch to do a screen test for Max later in the week. He handed Dutch the script of a Broadway play, *The Philadelphia Story*, and told him to memorize a part of it he liked. Dutch was glad not to have been asked to read something on the spot. Not only was he not wearing his glasses, but also even at the best of times he always sounded wooden when doing cold readings.

After the meeting with Bill, Dutch headed out to Catalina Island and the Cubs training camp. When he arrived, the team manager was angry with him for showing up a day late. For once, Dutch couldn't have cared less. His mind was on Hollywood and the lines he was learning for his screen test.

A few days later Dutch was back in Hollywood in front of a movie camera. He thought he had done a reasonable job at the screen test, but there was no way to tell for sure. The whole matter of who was hired as an actor at the studio rested with Jack Warner himself, and Warner never met the potential actors in person. He only reviewed the film of their screen test.

"We'll call you in a couple of days at the Biltmore," Max told Dutch when the screen test was over.

Dutch's heart sank. "I won't be there then. I'm leaving with the Cubs tomorrow. We're on our way back to Illinois for the season opener."

"But this is your chance, the chance you came here for. You can't blow it and leave now," Bill pleaded with Dutch when Max was out of earshot.

Dutch could not be dissuaded. He had come to meet with an agent, and he'd done much more than that. Now he would have to leave the rest in God's hands.

This was a bold stand, and one that Dutch regretted taking as the train rolled eastward across the Great Plains. What had he been thinking, telling the Warner Brothers casting director that he was too busy to be at his disposal! Yet what was done was done, and Dutch tried to concentrate on the Cubs upcoming season.

Dutch found it hard to settle into work his first day back at the radio station in Des Moines. Then just before lunch, the secretary dropped an envelope on his desk. Inside was a telegram that read, "WARNERS OFFERS CONTRACT SEVEN YEARS STOP ONE YEAR OPTION STOP STARTING $200 A WEEK STOP WHAT SHALL I DO MEIKLEJOHN."

Dutch read the telegram again and then let out a loud whoop. Everyone around turned to stare as Dutch cleared his throat and read the message aloud. A cheer went up, and everyone found it hard to work for the rest of the day. Dutch was so excited, he regaled everyone he could with stories about his screen test and imaginary tales of what lay ahead.

Later Dutch had a phone conversation with Bill, during which Bill gave him more details about the contract, which would start on June 1. This meant that Dutch had three months more to work at WHO and to wind up his affairs in Des Moines.

Dutch visited his parents in their tiny house in Dixon and promised them that as soon as he had saved enough money, he would send for them to come and live in California.

In April 1937, before he left Iowa, the Army insisted that Dutch take the medical exam to complete his training as a reserve cavalry officer. Reluctantly Dutch agreed, knowing that he would most likely not pass the eye test. However, he was aware of a technique that helped nearsighted people see a little better. Squinting an eye to a narrow slit allowed that eye to focus better and its vision to become sharper, thus allowing a person to see a little more than usual. Dutch practiced this technique when the army administered the eye test. He had to place his hand over one eye and read the chart with the other eye. Although nearsighted in both eyes, Dutch could see better in one of his eyes than the other. When he had to read the chart with his weaker eye, Dutch managed to create a small gap between the fingers of the hand he was holding over his good eye. In this way, with the aid of the squinting technique, he was able to read the chart with his good eye while pretending to read it with his bad eye. To his amazement he managed to pass the eye test. Dutch was commissioned as a private in the reserve cavalry, and less than a month later his rank was raised to second lieutenant.

On May 21, 1937, a farewell party was held for Dutch at Cy's Moonlight Club in Des Moines. Dutch thought of all the good times he'd had and the friends he'd made while living there, but most of all his thoughts were now on the future. What would he be doing five years from now? He surely hoped that he would be the biggest star of Western movies the world had ever seen.

Chapter 9

Hollywood

Dutch revved the engine of his Nash convertible and slowly let out the clutch. Soon he was cruising along at eighty miles an hour with the top down. The summer sun beat down, and the wind rushed through his hair. Dutch felt exhilarated; he was on his way to a new life as a movie actor. At twenty-six years of age, he was about to live his dream.

His dream started, however, with a sunburned face and raccoon eyes, since he had underestimated the power of the sun and the wind as he drove westward. Normally this would not have mattered, since no one saw Dutch on the radio. But now, for the first time, he realized that he would always have to be on guard about his appearance. He could not afford to be a sunburned star.

Upon his arrival in Los Angeles, Dutch checked into the Biltmore Hotel, where one of Bill Meiklejohn's assistants was waiting to greet him. Dutch was eager to know when he would start work, but the assistant told him that it could be weeks or even months before Warner Brothers got around to using his talent. This was a disappointment to Dutch, mainly because it pointed to the reality that here in Hollywood he was a small fish in a big pond.

Still, Dutch did not stay down for long. He cheered himself with the thought that at least he was in the pond and good things would happen for him if he put forth his best effort.

As it happened, it was not long before he got the opportunity to prove himself. Within just a few days, Jack Warner sent word that he had cast Dutch as the lead in *Love Is on the Air*. In this movie Dutch was to play Andy McCaine, the small-town radio announcer who stumbles upon the fact that his bosses are in partnership with the mob. When Andy tries to expose them, someone is murdered and Andy is demoted to children's radio before turning detective and figuring out who the murderer is.

The movie was due to start filming in four days. Dutch was astonished when he learned this, and even more astonished at what those four days entailed for him. It seemed to him that the studio wanted to transform him into someone quite different from the person they had hired, and they wanted it do it in four days! It began with his hair. Max Arnow told the hairstylist that it had to be changed; it was much too old-fashioned for Hollywood. That was easy to fix, compared to the next problem Max came up with. "His head is too small," he said.

Dutch gulped. No one had ever commented on the size of his head before.

"And his shoulders are too wide, and look at that short neck, totally out of proportion, totally wrong! Wardrobe!" Max bellowed. "See what you can do about his head."

Dutch took a deep breath and wondered, *what do they do here in Hollywood when they think a man's head is too small?* He was thankful that the answer did not involve any form of head stretching. The wardrobe woman told Dutch that one of their biggest stars, Jimmy Cagney, had the same problem of having a small head and short neck. But the wardrobe experts had come up with a specially designed shirt with a collar that made Cagney's neck look longer, and a set of similar shirts was ordered for Dutch.

Then the makeup department took a look at the young actor. Dutch knew what they would say—he had a deep ridge across the bridge of his nose that was made by his heavy glasses.

"What are we going to do with him?" the head makeup artist asked.

Dutch thought he now knew how a racehorse felt.

"We'll have to deemphasize as best we can," one of the makeup artists said as she sighed and shook her head. "Use darker makeup around the bridge of his nose. And turn those smile lines into dimples."

The next stop was the publicity department. Once again Dutch felt like an observer, as if he had nothing to do with what the five "experts" in the room with him were discussing. The conversation revolved around his name.

"Dutch Reagan...Dutch Reagan..." one of the Warner Brothers press agents said. "That's not right. We can't have a star named Dutch Reagan. What name does he look like?"

It was all Dutch could do not to interrupt the conversation, but he stayed silent.

"How about George? Does he look more like a George Defoe? Or a Hamilton Wiley? How about a David Torrey?"

Dutch stifled the urge to let out a nervous laugh. It was his identity they were talking about. He wondered how they would like it if someone randomly changed their names. Yet Dutch also knew that the names of many Hollywood stars were not their real names. For example, Edward G. Robinson was really Emmanuel Goldenberg, and Barbara Stanwyck's real name was Ruby Stevens. Now they wanted to come up with a new name for Dutch.

"How about something like Russell? Yes, we haven't had an R name for a while."

Dutch could contain himself no longer. "May I say something?" he asked.

The men turned to Dutch, looking at him as if they had totally forgotten he was in the room.

Dutch continued. "You may not know me here, but I must point out that I have a lot of name recognition in the Midwest, where I have been broadcasting sports. I think a lot of people would recognize my name on the theater marquees."

"But we couldn't possibly put Dutch Reagan on a marquee. It has no weight to it!" another of the press agents retorted.

Dutch could see his case was lost, and so was his name. In a split second he thought of an alternative that would be better than having a totally made-up name fostered on him.

"How about Ronald?" he asked. "Ronald Reagan?"

The men muttered the name among themselves a few times. "I kind of like the sound of that," one of them said.

"Not bad at all. Has a kind of ring to it," another agreed.

"Yes, let's go with Ronald Reagan," Max agreed and then added, "Good work, boys."

Dutch walked out of the publicity department using his legal name, Ronald Reagan. Only those who had known him before that time ever called him Dutch again.

That night Dutch, or Ron, as he now had to get used to being called, went back to his hotel in turmoil. He had three days left to prepare for the biggest role of his life, and he had not yet been given the script. This was because the writers were still writing it! Ron knew that he was not a good cold reader, especially without his glasses. He had to have the script ahead of time so that he could memorize it and make it his own.

The following day Ron spent hours at the wardrobe department preparing for the role of Andy McCaine.

Because B-rated actors like Ron were asked to provide their own clothes when they played a contemporary character, Ron brought two suits with him to the set. Both were approved for use in the movie. The wardrobe director decided that the polka-dot tie and Ron's class ring were perfect accessories. Ron chuckled to himself. Of course they were. He had worn them to work every day when he was a real radio announcer.

That night Ron checked out of the Biltmore Hotel and moved into the Montecito Apartments near Hollywood Boulevard. All the time he worried that he had not yet seen the script for the movie. The following day, Ron's worst fears were realized. Nick Grinde, the director of the movie, called the cast together, welcomed them to the set, and handed out copies of the script. "Okay, let's start the reading," he said.

The leading actress, June Travis, picked up her script and began reading with passion. Ron knew that he was in serious trouble. He could barely read the words, much less focus on what they meant.

A half hour later, the dialogue director pulled Ron aside. "Your screen test was so good, but now you can hardly get the words out," he said. "What's happened since you were here last?"

Ron knew that he had to tell the truth; it was his only chance. "I've never been any good at cold readings," he replied, knowing that all professional actors should be able to do them well. "But if you give me a little time to study the script, overnight for instance, I'll have it down perfectly for you tomorrow with all the feeling you could ask for."

The dialogue coach was taken aback. "Tomorrow will be your one and only shot. You blow that, and it's over," he said. "We'll move on to another shot that doesn't have you in it."

Ron was relieved. He knew that he could perform the lines well if he had time to work on them. He did nothing else that evening, and by the next day he was able to say all his lines with the right emotion. Ron was greatly relieved, and he suspected that the dialogue coach and director were also.

Ron had much to learn about making a movie, especially the different techniques required to act in front of a camera as opposed to acting before a live audience. He was grateful that his leading lady, June Travis, was already a veteran of over twenty films, and June gave him tips on how to act in many of the scenes. Ron wondered whether he would ever be able to say he'd made as many movies as June.

Work on *Love Is on the Air* went well, so well, in fact, that the filming wrapped up in three weeks, half the time allotted for a B-movie to be filmed. Everyone seemed to be happy with the result. With one movie under his belt, Ron waited to hear what his next assignment would be. This was an important matter. The fact that he had signed a seven-year contract with Warner Brothers did not mean that he would be paid to work for seven years straight or would even appear in one movie after another.

Ron was now part of a family of filmmakers that included actors, writers, musicians, directors, and producers bound for the length of their contract to Warner Brothers Studio. Under the terms of his

contract Ron was promised nineteen weeks of work
out of every twenty-six weeks, and for each of those
weeks he worked, he was paid two hundred dollars.
Any extra money he earned from making personal
appearances, being on the radio, or doing advertise-
ments was paid to the studio. And after four years of
his contract had expired, he had the right to renego-
tiate the contract.

Like the other big movie studios in Hollywood,
such as Metro-Goldwyn-Mayer (MGM) and Para-
mount, Warner Brothers not only produced movies but also had a chain of movie theaters in which
those movies were shown around the country. This,
of course, meant that the studio stayed busy making
films to show in its chain of movie theaters. Ron was
thankful that his next movie started just one week
after the completion of *Love Is on the Air.*

The new movie was called *Sergeant Murphy,* and
once again Ron played the leading role. This time he
played Private Dennis Reilley, a timid young man
who joins the army to be with his best friend, Sergeant Murphy, who happens to be a horse. When
Private Reilley is about to get out of the army, he
wants his friend (the horse) to come with him. To do
so he has to find a way to get the horse kicked out
of the army. Private Reilley succeeds and trains Sergeant Murphy to be a champion racer. He manages
to sneak the horse into England to race in the British Grand National, which the horse wins.

Ron was delighted not only to have another
starring role in a movie so soon but also to have
a role where he got to ride a horse. He was even

more delighted when it was revealed that much of the movie would be filmed at an outdoor location on the Monterey Peninsula in California. Ron fell in love with the area as soon as he saw it. The scenery on the peninsula was spectacular, with large, unobstructed views of the Pacific Ocean. The town of Monterey at the southern end of Monterey Bay, where the cast stayed during filming, was full of Old Mexico charm. The streets were lined with adobe buildings sporting red-tiled roofs, while docks lined the oceanfront, where, after filming, the cast would visit with the local fishermen. To Ron, it was all so different from Illinois or Iowa.

When filming for *Sergeant Murphy* was complete, *Love Is on the Air* had been released to movie theaters. Ron heaved a great sigh of relief when he read the favorable reviews of the film.

After *Sergeant Murphy,* more roles followed. Sometimes Ron played the lead in the movie, and sometimes he just made a brief appearance. Along the way he played a small-town entertainment promoter, a sportscaster, an announcer, and a navy flyer.

The filming of movies was done at a fast clip, and by the time the last scenes of his next movie were shot, *Sergeant Murphy* had hit the big screen. Once again, the reviews were positive, positive enough for Jack Warner to offer Ron a pay raise to $250 a week for a minimum of sixteen weeks of work over the next six months.

Ron was thrilled. Now he had the financial stability he needed to bring his parents out to California.

He sent them train tickets for the journey and rented them a small apartment in West Hollywood, a central location that he knew his mother would enjoy. Buses regularly ran past the place, and the Hollywood-Beverly Christian Church was within walking distance.

Ron met his parents when they arrived at Union Station in Los Angeles. He was shocked at how much his father had aged. Jack had lost the use of his left hand, which was now clawed up, giving him a frightening look. Still, Ron was glad when his mother took him aside to say that his father had not had a drink in a long while.

Nelle beamed as they pulled up in front of their new apartment, and Ron knew it had all been worthwhile when he saw the look on his mother's face. Although his parents had never before been west of the Rocky Mountains, Ron was confident that his mother would find some poor souls who needed her help and that his father would follow along.

As for Ron, he had a steady stream of movie roles ahead of him. None of them appeared to be the record-shattering one he would have liked to be in, but they were movie roles nonetheless.

Meanwhile, Nelle admired the Christmas ornaments on Hollywood Boulevard, and as the family celebrated the coming of 1938 together, Ron had every reason to believe that their lives would continue to improve. He longed to break into A-movies and felt that 1938 could well be the year it happened.

All American

The Amazing Dr. Clitterhouse, Boy Meets Girl, Girls on Probation—the B-movie credits kept coming. Ron was grateful for the work. After all, he had his parents to fully support now, but he was anxious for his big break. That break came in the form of a movie with the unlikely name of *Brother Rat*. Brother Rat was the nickname cadets at the Virginia Military Institute used for each other, and the movie was about three Rats: Bing Edwards, who was constantly getting into trouble; Billy Randolf; and Dan Crawford, Bing's loyal and easygoing friend who was always shocked at the situations the three got themselves into. Ron was cast in the role of Dan Crawford.

Although most of the cast members were relative newcomers to Hollywood, in Ron's eyes they all seemed very experienced. Ron was particularly drawn to Jane Wyman, who played his character's girlfriend, Claire Adams. Jane had been in Hollywood two years longer than Ron and, like Ron, had come from small-town America roots. She had grown up in St. Joseph, Missouri, and Cleveland, Ohio. Her home life, however, had been more tumultuous than Ron's. Her parents had divorced when she was about five years old, and Jane had been given to an older couple, Richard and Emma Fulks, to be raised. Although never legally adopted by the couple, she went by the name Sarah Jane Fulks.

Jane had always dreamed of being an actress and had worked as a radio singer along the way. When she got to Hollywood, the studios changed her name to Jane Wyman.

Soon the former Dutch and Sarah—now Ron and Jane—were a steady couple. Ron found Jane attractive, with her doelike brown eyes and bobbed, blonde hairdo.

After the release of *Brother Rat,* Ron and Jane waited anxiously for the reviews. On November 5, 1938, a review appeared in *The New York Times.* "The Warners have filled the vacancies with a mettlesome troupe of juniors. Wayne Morris, Ronald Reagan, Jane Wyman, Priscilla Lane, Johnnie Davis, Jane Bryan, William Tracey, and the others discharged their duties so amiably that we won't bother to single out the best of them, but invite them to share a bow."

Ron was pleased with the review and hoped that it would help him land some better acting jobs. But for some reason that Ron could never figure out, the good review did not help as much as he thought it would. Warner Brothers continued to cast him for roles in B-movies. Meanwhile, Ron and Jane were being dubbed the celebrity couple to watch. They appeared to have the ultimate glamorous lifestyle, but, in fact, things were a lot more mundane than they appeared.

Jane loved Nelle Reagan's stable, pious ways, and the two women became close. Jane was impressed with the way that Nelle was always reaching out to help needy people. Nelle's capacity for giving of herself seemed boundless.

In early September 1939, Ron read in the newspaper that war had broken out in Europe, with Germany fighting Great Britain and France.

Also in the fall of 1939, Ron and Jane were part of a Hollywood tour group sent across the country to promote a new variety show. The itinerary called for them to fly from San Francisco to Philadelphia on a small chartered airplane. But things did not go well. The plane found itself in the midst of a blinding snowstorm, and everyone aboard feared for the worst. Ron, seeing that panic could quickly take over, led the group in a sing-a-long. His action seemed to calm everyone's nerves as the plane made an emergency landing in Chicago.

Everyone walked away from the plane unhurt, but Ron was exhausted. He never wanted to go through such an experience again, and he promised himself that he was done with flying. If he couldn't get there by car or ship or train, he did not need to go.

The remainder of the trip was uneventful except for the stop in New York City, where Ron and Jane decided to get engaged. The troupe returned to Hollywood in the middle of January 1940. It was a new year and a new start for Ron and Jane.

The couple were married on January 26, 1940, at the Wee Kirk o' the Heather wedding chapel in Glendale. Ron's Christian Church pastor officiated at the service. The event was a big Hollywood affair, with the press referring to it as a fairytale wedding. Jane looked stunning in a pale blue satin gown, complete with a mink hat. Ron wore a dark blue suit with a white carnation in his lapel.

Ron was happy to be in love with and now married to such a beautiful woman. He looked forward to creating a home and having children with Jane. His part of the American dream was coming true.

After the wedding and reception, the newlyweds drove in Ron's new car to Palm Springs for their honeymoon. When they returned to Hollywood, Ron moved into Jane's apartment. It was a definite upgrade. The apartment at 1326 Londonderry View, with two bathrooms and three bedrooms, overlooked Sunset Strip. Ron turned the third bedroom into his office.

Ron and Jane also officially joined the Hollywood-Beverly Christian Church, something Ron had neglected to do up until this point, and Jane started teaching Sunday school classes at the church.

Jane was an avid golfer, and Ron eagerly took up her sport. Together they applied for membership at the Lakeside Country Club and soon found out that

Jack Warner had applied to join at the same time. It came as a shock to Ron when he learned that Jack Warner's application was rejected because Jack was Jewish. One thing that Ron could not tolerate was any form of discrimination, and he immediately withdrew his application to join the country club. He did not want to play golf in a Gentiles-only club.

Ron knew about the terrible treatment that the Jews in Germany were suffering at the hands of the Nazi government, but he did not expect Jews to be discriminated against in the United States. Ron and Jane joined the Hillcrest Country Club at Beverly Hills. This club accepted Jewish members. Soon the Reagans were firm friends with celebrities much more famous than they, including Jack Benny, George Burns, and Gracie Allen.

Ron and Jane were cast in several more movies together, including *An Angel from Texas* and *The Butter and Egg Man*. During this time Ron became intrigued with his wife's involvement in the Screen Actor's Guild, or SAG, as it was referred to. He had been a member of the guild since arriving in Hollywood as an actor, but he had never really bothered to understand how the organization worked or why it existed. Jane, on the other hand, had been an active member of SAG from the beginning of her career, and she served on several of the guild's committees. Ron found himself curious as to the inner workings and the role that SAG played, and he began attending their meetings.

By now Ron's brother Moon had married, and he and his wife, Bess, had also moved to Hollywood.

Ron knew that his mother loved having her two sons in one place again, but the new arrangement put pressure on Ron. Moon expected his brother to help him break into show business. Ron did what he could, and Moon was cast in a small role.

With the steady income from his career, Ron was able to buy a two-bedroom stucco house for his parents. This was the first house they had ever owned, and they were very proud of it. Ron also talked his bosses at Warner Brothers into giving his father a part-time job sorting Ron's fan mail and replying to it. This helped Jack Reagan feel less dependent on his successful son.

Meanwhile, Ron decided to become more proactive about his movie roles. The roles he really wanted to play were not coming his way, and Jane challenged him to create his own opportunities. Ron took her advice to heart and thought about the kinds of roles he would really love to play. He thought a role about a football hero would be perfect. But where was that role?

A football star who came to mind was George Gipp. Ron was acquainted with Gipp's college football career with Notre Dame. Gipp was a spectacular and versatile player who had helped lead his team to many victories. During his senior year, however, soon after being elected All-American player, Gipp had died from viral pneumonia. George Gipp's story was exciting and motivational and was the kind of role Ron would love to play in a movie. Taking his wife's advice, Ron started talking to writers and directors at Warner Brothers about George Gipp's story in the hope of getting someone interested in making a movie about the man. Despite Ron's best effort, no one seemed interested.

Then one day Ron was reading *Variety Magazine*, and he could barely believe what he read. Warner Brothers was planning to make a movie about the life of Knute Rockne, with Pat O'Brien playing the lead role. Knute Rockne was the famous Notre Dame football coach who was killed in a plane crash in 1931. Knute Rockne had also been George Gipp's coach.

Back at the studio, Ron found out all he could about the upcoming production. He could hardly contain his excitement when he learned that the role of George Gipp had not yet been cast. This was a plum role, and Ron wanted it. He spoke to the movie's producer, Hal Wallis, who was skeptical. Wallis told Ron that the young actor did not look the strong football type. Ron pointed out to the producer that Gipp weighed only five pounds less than Ron. Ron left the studio, drove home to collect a photograph of himself on the field dressed in his football gear as part of the Golden Tornadoes football team at Eureka College, and an hour later was showing the picture to Wallis. Hal Wallis seemed to have a change of heart after seeing the photo, because he let Ron try out for the role. Much to his delight, Ron was cast to play George Gipp in the movie, *Knute Rockne All American.*

Soon Ron was busy learning his lines and preparing for the movie, some of which was shot in the studio in Hollywood. A number of scenes were filmed at Notre Dame in South Bend, Indiana. There on the football field at Notre Dame, decked out in a football uniform, Ron for a short while got to be the football star that he never managed to be on his high school or college team. Ron kicked, passed, and caught the ball. He broke through tackles and ran over opponents as he made touchdown after touchdown, all with the cameras rolling and under the careful control of the movie's director, Lloyd Bacon.

In one of the most poignant scenes in the movie, Ron gave the role his all. In the scene George Gipp (Ron) is lying in a hospital bed about to die from viral pneumonia. Knute Rockne is at his side as Gipp whispers his last words: "Someday, when the team's up against it, breaks are beating the boys, ask them to go in there with all they've got. Win one for the Gipper." Little did Ron know at the time that these would become the most memorable lines he ever uttered as an actor.

Ron was proud of his role in *Knute Rockne All American.* He told people that he suspected that many other actors in Hollywood could have played the part better, but none could have wanted it more than he did.

Knute Rockne All American was scheduled for release in September 1940. Jack Warner had decided that the best place to premier the movie was at Notre Dame in conjunction with a football game. When she heard this, Nelle Reagan asked Ron to take his father along for the festivities. Jack Reagan's health was failing fast, and as an Irish-Catholic, Jack dreamed of one day seeing the Notre Dame football

team play. Ron was reluctant to agree. His father
had sworn off alcohol since before moving to California, but Ron was concerned about what might
happen to his father's resolve if he were surrounded
by so many heavy drinkers. Still, Ron could not turn
down his mother's request, and he asked Jack Warner to make arrangements for his father to travel
with the publicity team to Notre Dame.

Jane had just learned that she was pregnant.
She was also hard at work on a film of her own, and
did not travel with Ron to Indiana.

The premier event at Notre Dame proved to be
everything that Ron dreamed it would be. Huge
crowds met the cast members at Union Station in
South Bend. These celebrities were bringing the
men who were their local heroes to national attention. Press conferences were held, as were a ban-
quet, a luncheon with the mayor, and a grand ball
at the Palais Royal Hotel. President Roosevelt's son
Franklin Jr. attended the event and read a letter of
congratulations from the president.

Jack Reagan was in his element, whether ban-
tering with the college's mother superior, Bob Hope,
or the current players on the Notre Dame football
team. Sadly, Ron's fears were realized, and Ron's
father was not able to resist the whiskey bottle.

The event culminated with a football game
between the College of the Pacific and Notre Dame.
What a game it turned out to be! Ron was asked
to step back into his old role as Dutch Reagan and
announce the first fifteen minutes of the second half
of the game. Of course, Ron loved the opportunity to

be back in the press box, speaking into the micro-phone. Excitement mounted as Notre Dame came from behind to win the game with a touchdown in the final minutes.

When the game was over, the group climbed aboard the train and headed back west. As they trav-eled, Jack Reagan told Ron that he could now die a happy man; he'd had the best weekend of his life.

Fort Roach

Jane gave birth to a daughter on January 4, 1941. Ron and Jane gave the baby a good Irish name, Maureen Elizabeth Reagan. Soon after the baby's arrival, Ron and Jane realized that their apartment was now too small, so they bought a lot on a steep hill overlooking the Pacific Ocean. Jane watched over the construction of an eight-room house on the property while still pursuing her acting career. Ron paid less attention to such domestic matters. His attention, like that of so many others in the United States, was on Great Britain and other parts of Europe.

The war in Europe raged on. The Germans had overrun France and put in place a puppet government. Constant German air raids had battered Great Britain, reducing parts of London to rubble. In addition, the Germans and Italians and the Japanese in the Far East had formed an alliance known as the Axis. As a result, the war had now spread to North Africa and East Asia. Ron agreed with President Roosevelt, who believed that Great Britain could not be allowed to fall into the hands of the Germans and that the United States needed to rally to help the British. But Congress was reluctant to commit the United States to involvement in a war in Europe. Nonetheless, Ron did not hold back on giving his opinion to anyone who wanted to listen to him on what the United States should do.

On May 18, 1941, Jack Reagan died of a heart attack. He was sixty years old. Ron was saddened by the death of his father yet comforted by the thought of the wonderful time his father had enjoyed at Notre Dame just months earlier.

Soon after Ron's father's death, Jack Warner loaned Ron to Metro-Goldwyn-Mayer to appear in a movie the studio was making called *The Bad Man.* This was allowable under the terms of the contract Ron had signed with Warner Brothers. Ron was angry when he learned that Warner Brothers was being paid two thousand dollars a week for his services while he pocketed only five hundred dollars a week. Still, Ron could do nothing about what he considered to be an unjust arrangement.

More movie roles followed for Ron, and more premiers. In the fall of 1941, Ron was cast in a big-budget movie called *Kings Row.* Ron played the role of Drake McHugh as the melodrama wound its way through lost fortunes and poisonings and culminated with Drake having both his legs amputated by a crazed surgeon on a moral mission. When Drake awakes from his amputation, he utters the words "Where's the rest of me?" Ron had practiced the words so many times before the scene was filmed that people close to him never forgot them and often joked with him about them.

While acting in *Kings Row*, Ron experimented with an entirely new device—contact lenses. He hated wearing his glasses so much that he was prepared to try any new invention that would help. The contact lenses were made of glass and plastic and covered the entire eye—cornea and the whites. Each lens had a section that had to be filled with liquid, which turned gray and cloudy every few hours. This meant that Ron was constantly taking his lenses out, rinsing them, refilling them with liquid, and putting them back in. It was a lot of bother, but Ron did not mind. It was worth it to him to see without wearing his thick glasses.

Both Ron and Jane continued with their acting careers as the war in Europe grew more frightening. Germany continued to take over more and more countries in Europe, while the British staunchly held on in the face of German bombardment from the air.

By now the Reagans had moved into their dream house on the hill overlooking both the Pacific Ocean and the City of Los Angeles. The house had a large swimming pool and picture windows that allowed them to enjoy the view below.

On December 7, 1941, Ron was taking an early afternoon nap when Jane awoke him. She insisted that he come into the living room and listen to the radio. The news was unbelievable: Japan had bombed Pearl Harbor in Hawaii. This was the first attack on U.S. soil, and the nation was stunned. With one air raid, everything changed. The following day President Franklin Roosevelt declared war on Japan.

Jane thought that Ron might be called up for active military service in the war, but Ron knew the chances of that were slim. He had recently taken another physical to update his reserve cavalry files and had been flagged because of his poor eyesight. That, combined with the fact he had a small child, meant that under normal circumstances he would not be sent to active duty. But more important, Jack Warner assured Ron that the paperwork was already in the works to get Ron a deferment from any military service so that he could keep making movies.

Sure enough, Ron was granted a three-month deferment, and he kept busy making movies. The war brought a big change to Warner Brothers, and the studio began turning out war movie after war movie. Ron starred in one of them, *Desperate Journey*.

When Jack Warner applied for an extension to Ron's deferment to finish *Desperate Journey*, Ron was not so lucky. The telegram he received was brief and to the point:

REGRET TO INFORM YOU THAT ANOTHER DEFERMENT CANNOT BE GRANTED 2ND LT. RONALD WILSON REAGAN CAVALRY STOP SHORTAGE OF AVAILABLE OFFICERS

PREVENTS FAVORABLE CONSIDERATION—
HORACE SKYES, COLONEL AGD, ADJ. GEN-
ERAL, FT. DOUGLAS, UTAH.

On April 19, 1942, Ron reported for duty at Fort
Mason, California, near San Francisco. A new phase
of his life had begun.

Warner Brothers had worked feverishly to finish filming Ron's scenes for *Desperate Journey*. And
before he left Hollywood, Ron had done everything
he could to ease the financial burden on Jane and
his mother. While in the army, Ron would no longer
receive his Warner Brothers salary. The family would
have to survive on Jane's salary and whatever he got
paid by the army. Ron went over the family budget
and legal papers with Jane and took out a loan so
that his mother could receive seventy-five dollars a
week to cover her expenses for a year. The thing Ron
hated most about going was leaving behind fifteen-
month-old Maureen. Ron was not sure when he
would see her or Jane or his mother again.

The first order when Ron arrived at his posting was a complete physical. Ron, who was in good
physical shape, passed the exam with flying colors,
except for his eyesight. The two doctors present mar-
veled at how he had managed to sneak by the test
in the first place to become a reserve officer. "If we
sent you overseas, you'd shoot at a general," one of
the doctors quipped. "And," the other added, "you'd
probably miss!"

Because there was no way that Ron could
be posted overseas to fight, he was placed on the

domestic roster. For the next two months he trained alongside other cavalry officers, and then most of them were shipped off to the Pacific front. In the meantime Ron waited to find out what would happen to him. He was a cavalry officer, and the cavalry was part of the U.S. Army, as was the U.S. Air Force. Before he knew it, Ron had been transferred to the Air Force and sent to serve at Fort Roach.

General Henry "Hap" Arnold, the commanding general of the Army Air Force, had realized the impact that motion pictures could have on training and morale. He thus had created the First Motion Picture Unit, which was located at the old Hal Roach Studios in Culver City on the outskirts of Hollywood. The unit had soon become known as either the Roach Unit or Fort Wacky, depending upon who was speaking.

When Ron arrived to take up his post with the First Motion Picture Unit, he realized that he had been assigned to probably the strangest military group ever assembled. Thirteen hundred men and officers, all with movie production backgrounds, were gathered together. Actors like Ron, directors, set designers, cameramen, grips, sound recorders, film editors, and the like were all ready to make training films for the Army Air Force. Soon Fort Roach was turning out all sorts of instructional films, from how to fly a bomber to how to fire a rifle and everything in between.

Within weeks, Ron was involved in another film. The movie, *The Rear Gunner,* was a documentary-style drama on the training of aerial rear gunners for the war. Ron was to be the narrator for the movie. It was a strange experience for him and many of the other men to be making a movie while being on active military service. The men still had to report in and out to work, ask permission to go to the latrine, and salute their superiors. This last rule led to some amusing incidents as enlisted men tried to figure out whether the man with the stripes on his uniform really was a lieutenant or captain or was merely an actor in costume. Eventually, the army solved this problem by ordering all "fake" officers to wear special armbands when the cameras were not rolling.

Ron went on to make other movies for the army and review thousands of hours of war footage. Some of the things he saw were top secret and were used to help train bomber flight crews to identify specific landmarks from the air.

This work was satisfying, and Ron felt that he was making the best contribution he could to the war effort. He tried to assuage his guilt at not being overseas on the frontlines. He knew that even if he were not a movie star, because of his poor eyesight, he would never have been sent overseas. As the war years rolled on, Ron remained assigned to the First Motion Picture Unit.

During early February 1945, newly reelected President Franklin Roosevelt, British Prime Minister Winston Churchill, and Secretary General Joseph Stalin of the Soviet Union met in a conference in Yalta on the Crimean Peninsula. The purpose of the conference was to oversee the dividing up of postwar Europe, since the war in Europe looked like it was nearly over. For Ron, as for most Americans, the war had ground on for much longer than he had ever imagined it would, and the prospect of the end of the war approaching was a relief.

Throughout his posting to Fort Roach, Ron was able to get home frequently to visit Jane and Maureen and check up on his mother. Everything seemed to be fine. Jane was busy working, as the war had spurred a boom in movie attendance in the United States. It seemed that many Americans at home wanted some way to escape the constant talk of war.

With the war winding down, Ron and Jane began to discuss their family. Both of them wanted more children, and they decided to find a needy child to adopt. Maureen was four years old when Michael Reagan was born on March 14, 1945, and was brought home to the Reagans four days later. Ron was there to meet Michael and help Maureen adjust to her new brother. Not that the new baby took much adjusting to. Maureen had been nagging her parents for a baby brother for over a year and even had a piggybank filled with pennies to help "buy" one. When the woman from the adoption agency arrived at the house with a real baby brother, Maureen was wide-eyed with excitement. She rushed upstairs to get her piggybank so that she could pay the adoption agency.

Ron went back to Fort Roach a jubilant new father and a captain, the rank to which he had been newly promoted. It felt wonderful to him to have a son and a civilian future ahead.

A month after Michael's adoption, on April 12, 1945, President Franklin Roosevelt died. An invalid for much of his life, he had given all of his energy to guiding the United States through the war. Vice President Harry Truman was sworn in as thirty-third President of the United States. As Ron watched the news coverage of the event, he felt sad. President Roosevelt had been his hero and had come so close to living to see the United States at peace once again.

The war in Europe drew to an end with the surrender of Germany on May 7, 1945. This wonderful news, however, was overshadowed by the fact that Japan continued to fight in Asia and the Pacific. Then on August 6, an American bomber dropped an atomic bomb on the Japanese city of Hiroshima. Three days later another atomic bomb was dropped, this time on Nagasaki. The devastating explosions finally brought the Japanese to their knees, and they surrendered eight days later on August 15, 1945.

Captain Ronald Reagan had been honorably discharged from the army on July 11, 1945, a month before the war officially came to an end. Now that he was no longer in the army, Ron wanted to spend time with his wife and children, but things did not go smoothly. Jane had just been cast in a big-budget film called *The Yearling,* in which she starred alongside Gregory Peck and Claude Jarman Jr. Jane played the role of Orry Baxter, a hardworking pioneer wife who had buried three of her children. Because of this, Orry was haunted by the idea that her one remaining child might die. The role was sad and grueling to play, and Jane found it hard to shake off her depressed state when she came home from the set late at night. Then she would have to leave again at five o'clock in the morning. Ron saw plenty of Maureen and baby Michael, but he hardly saw his wife. Postwar life was turning out to be not as idyllic as he had hoped it would be.

Chapter 12

SAG

Financially, Ron was doing fine. Warner Brothers upped his contract to one million dollars over the next seven years, and Jane was making good money in her movies. But as a result of a series of circumstances that had nothing to do with Ron, he was not cast immediately in any film roles. Restless and wanting to be busy, Ron immersed himself in the Screen Actors Guild (SAG). He had belonged to the guild before and during the war and had served on the board for a while. Now that he was discharged from the army, he began serving again on the guild's board.

Ron was particularly interested in understanding the role that the guild and unions played in postwar America. What he found out was startling. Each union member gave two percent of his or her income to belong to the union, and that added up to big money. Money meant power, and power meant politics.

Ron read long into the night and attended dozens of meetings to try to figure out the internal workings of many unions. Hundreds of people were involved in the making of a movie, and they represented a wide range of industries and crafts. There were people who did the makeup, sewed the costumes, built the sets, painted the backdrops, manned the cameras, rigged the lighting, and performed a whole host of other tasks. All of these people belonged to various unions, and these unions, along with SAG, belonged to the much larger American Federation of Labor (AFL).

Many of those who worked for the movie studios were blue-collar workers earning low wages, particularly those who built the sets for movies. In an attempt to increase the wages for these workers, the AFL voted to strike. However, SAG was against the strike because it would put many people, including actors, out of work. This stance put the guild at odds with the AFL. The decision not to support a strike also split SAG down the middle. Ron found himself on the conservative side of the split, arguing that jobs were the most important thing, while other prominent actors on the liberal side believed that a workingman needed help from the unions or the government to keep his job.

Faced with a looming strike, SAG appointed Ron to head an emergency committee to try to head off a strike at the movie studios. Ron and a group of others from the Screen Actors Guild flew to Chicago to meet with William Green, the AFL's president. Ron thought the job was so important that he overcame his fear of flying and agreed to once again step into an airplane.

The meeting with William Green was an eye-opener. Ron had hoped to have a reasoned conversation with the man, but instead he found Green to be an arrogant bully who was not interested in any dissenting opinion. Green insisted that the strike would go ahead.

A meeting with William Hutcheson, the leader of the carpenters union, which represented many of the blue-collar workers at the studios, produced a similar result. Ron was shocked to hear Hutcheson's parting words: "There'll be only one man running labor in Hollywood, and that man will be me!"

So much for working together to build a stronger, postwar America, Ron thought as he returned home to Hollywood. He'd had a glimpse of the *real* powers that manipulated workers, and he did not like what he saw. For the first time in his life, Ron found himself examining his allegiance to the liberal Democratic stance that Franklin Roosevelt had modeled.

The dispute between the unions and the studios became more heated, and still SAG refused to strike. Since Ron was the head of SAG's emergency committee and the one who had done most of the negotiating with William Green, much of the anger of the unions was leveled at him. One day while filming on the set, Ron was called to the telephone. "Hello?" Ron said, putting the receiver to his ear.

A gruff voice on the other end of the line said, "We'll mess up that pretty face of yours so that you will never work again in front of a camera."

Although Ron did not recognize the voice on the phone, there was no doubting the threat. Union leaders were prepared to do him physical harm if he did not back their call for a strike. But Ron was undeterred. He would not be coerced into backing away from the stand he and SAG had taken regarding a strike. However, he did start to carry a small pistol on him at all times in case someone tried to deliver on the threat.

Ron was relieved when eventually the problems with the AFL blew over, but another challenge lay ahead. A deep-rooted fear had begun to take hold in the country, fueled by a fear of the Soviet Union. Some Americans began to suspect that the Soviets were secretly trying to subvert American democracy and turn the country into a Communist state.

Ron saw firsthand the power that this fear could have over people when a lawyer named Richard Nixon decided to campaign for a seat in the U.S. Congress. Nixon's popular Democratic opponent had already served five terms as a congressman, and it was expected that he would easily win reelection—that is, until Nixon began making inflammatory statements about his opponent siding with Communist sympathizers. No evidence was produced that this was, in fact, the truth, and none seemed to have been needed, as Richard Nixon beat his opponent and was elected to the Congress.

Another politician also seized on this fear of Communists. He was J. Parnell Thomas, a Republican congressman from New Jersey. Thomas began to gain national attention when he started making claims that Hollywood was filled with Communist sympathizers and that many of the movies produced by the Hollywood studios were leftist propaganda.

FBI agents came to Hollywood to investigate these allegations. One evening they came to Ron's house to visit him. They asked questions about the Screen Actors Guild and whether Ron believed that the organization was infiltrated by Communists. Ron agreed that yes, probably a small percentage of members of the guild were Communist or at least very left-leaning in their politics, and he gave to the FBI agents the names of those he suspected. But he also took pains to point out that SAG was a democratic organization that followed the majority vote of its members, and that ninety-nine percent of the members of the guild were fine, upstanding Americans who had the good of their country at heart and were in no way subversives.

While Ron was heavily involved in SAG, life went on around him. Ron made a movie called *Stallion Road*, not one of his best pictures. However, in the course of filming it he got to ride a beautiful black stallion with the stage name Tar Baby. Ron fell in love with the horse and did all of the jumps and other stunts the movie called for. When filming of the movie was finished, Ron bought Tar Baby and a partnership in a small ranch on which to stable the horse.

Ron's next movie, a film whose story Ron strongly disagreed with, turned out to be a publicity disaster. In *That Hagen Girl*, he played the part of Tom Bates, a thirty-six-year-old man who falls in love with seventeen-year-old Mary Hagen, played by Shirley Temple. Shirley Temple was a famous, curly-haired child actress who, at nineteen years of age, was starring in her first adult movie role.

When Ron read the script for the movie, he was appalled. Ron did everything he could to get out of acting in the movie, but Jack Warner was adamant: Ron was under contract to the studio, and he would act in the movie as per his contract. Ron could not imagine the public approving of the story. When he could not get out of acting in the movie, he begged Jack Warner to change the script. Jack Warner would have none of it.

At the same time he was battling with Jack Warner over his role in *That Hagen Girl*, Ron was elected president of the Screen Actors Guild. Now with his duties as president and a new movie to act in, Ron was busier than ever.

Even though Jane was pregnant with their third child, the gap between her and Ron was becoming obvious to everyone, and the media played on it. Since the end of the war, better roles were being written for leading ladies. Jane had won one of the best of these roles, that of Belinda MacDonald in the movie *Johnny Belinda*. In the movie, Jane's character was a deaf-mute who was hated by her father and misunderstood by her community. Jane threw herself into the demanding role, often spending hours at a time with plugs in her ears to capture the feeling of being deaf.

Filming of *That Hagen Girl* began in June 1947. The script called for Ron's character, Tom Drake, to jump into a river to save Mary Hagen. The filming for this scene started on June 18. The water in the river was freezing cold, and Ron, summoning memories of his lifeguard days at Lowell Park in Dixon, Illinois, refused a stunt double for the action sequence. In the end he had to jump into the frigid river seven times until the director was satisfied that he had the best take of the scene. The next morning Ron awoke with a sore throat and fever. The symptoms quickly progressed to viral pneumonia, the same illness that had killed George Gipp, his character in *Knute Rockne All American*. Ron was barely conscious when he was loaded into an ambulance and whisked off to Cedars of Lebanon Hospital.

The next day his mother came to see him in the hospital. Nelle had some sad news for her son. After Ron had been taken to the hospital, Jane went into premature labor and had been taken to Queen of Angels Hospital. The three-month premature baby, a girl whom Jane named Christine, had lived through the night in an incubator but had died that morning. Ron knew that Jane needed him now more than ever, but he was helpless to do anything. He was deathly ill himself.

A week passed by before Ron was well enough to go home. By the time he got home, Jane had slipped into a deep depression. Ron wished that he could spend more time with his wife, but he had to get right back to filming *That Hagen Girl,* and his SAG work was as demanding and complicated as ever.

With the completion of filming, *That Hagen Girl* was rushed through production and premiered in New York City on October 24, 1947. *The New York Times* did its customary advance review of the movie. The review was as bad as Ron imagined it would be. He cringed as he read it.

The following day, October 25, 1947, Ron was in Washington, D.C. He had been subpoenaed, along with George Murphy and Robert Montgomery, to testify before the House Un-American Activities Committee. Congressman J. Parnell Thomas was now the chairman of this committee and was using his position to continue his investigation—some called it a witch hunt—into the infiltration of Hollywood by Communist sympathizers and activists.

In the days preceding, Jack Warner, Walt Disney, and Louis B. Mayer of the Metro-Goldwyn-Mayer Studio had all testified before the committee. Nineteen other men accused of being agents of un-American propaganda in the film industry had been subpoenaed to testify after Ron.

George Murphy, a member of the SAG board of directors, and then Robert Montgomery, the previous president of the guild, were the first to testify. Each man answered the questions put to him, stating that perhaps one percent of the SAG members could be Communist sympathizers but that the guild itself was a very democratic and nonsubversive organization. Neither man reported to the committee the names of anyone in the guild who they might consider a Communist sympathizer or agent.

At 11:10 AM Ron was called to take the oath before the House Un-American Activities Committee. Ron wore his glasses and a beige suite. He took his place in the chair behind the microphone and studied the faces of the committee members. It was his first opportunity to see J. Parnell Thomas face-to-face. The committee chairman was a pale-faced, flabby man who sat at a desk above the other committee members at the front of the dark wood–paneled committee room. A pool of photographers squatted on the floor and snapped pictures of Ron as he pre-pared to answer the committee's questions.

Soon the questions began. Ron answered them as best he could and asserted that George Murphy and Robert Montgomery had answered the questions well and that there was not much more he could add to their answers.

Then Robert Stripling, the chief investigator for the committee, asked Ron, "Mr. Reagan, what is your feeling about what steps should be taken to rid the motion picture industry of any Communist influences, if they are there?"

Ron started his answer by reiterating that he did not believe that SAG was particularly infiltrated by Communists, but he believed that SAG was a very democratic organization. Then he said:

> Fundamentally I would say in opposing those people [Communist sympathizers] that the best thing to do is to make democracy work. In the Screen Actors Guild we make it work by insuring everyone a vote and by keeping everyone informed. I believe that, as Thomas Jefferson put it, if all American people know all of the facts they will never make a mistake.
>
> Whether the [Communist] party should be outlawed, I agree with the gentlemen that pre-ceded me that that is a matter for the government to decide. As a citizen I would hesitate, or not like, to see any political party outlawed on the basis of its political ideology. We have

> spent 170 years in this country on the basis
> that democracy is strong enough to stand up
> and fight against the inroads of any ideology.

The following day Ron headed back to Hollywood by
train.

On November 1, *That Hagen Girl* opened in movie
theaters across the United States. It was the low point
of Ron's career, and it happened just as Jane Wyman's
career was hitting a new high point. Somewhere
along the way—with the death of the baby, Ron's illness, both of their busy schedules making movies,
and Ron's SAG work—Ron and Jane's marriage had
been lost. As a result, Jane filed for divorce.

Ron was stunned. He knew that things between
them were not going well and that Jane had been
depressed, but he came from small-town America
where divorce was seldom an option.

Jane went to New York to visit friends, and Ron
hoped that when she returned to Hollywood the two
of them could reconcile. But it was not to be. The
divorce was finalized on June 29, 1948. Their dream
house on the hill was sold, and Jane and the children moved to Malibu. Ron's old apartment was up
for rent again, and he moved back into it.

Ron was heartbroken by the divorce. He had
always wanted a family, and now that dream lay in
tatters. He threw himself into his work as president
of the Screen Actors Guild. A relatively new invention, television, had moved Hollywood into what Ron
described as a revolution.

In his lifetime, Ron had seen movies progress
from silent films to talking pictures. Most were still

filmed in black and white, but more and more color movies were being made. All of these developments were predictable—inevitable—and the same contracts could cover them all. But now that television had come along, Ron could envisage the time when there would be a television set in every home. And when that happened, there would be a big demand for movies intended for the big screen of the movie theater to be played on television.

The big question was, who should get the money that the television stations would pay to broadcast the movies? The movie producers argued that they should get the money because they had bought the actors' time and skill and so they owned the movie. The actors, represented by the Screen Actors Guild, disagreed. They argued that when they had signed contracts to make movies, they were not signing away their television rights, because television did not exist at the time. So now they wanted a share of the profits made when their work was shown on television.

The struggle over who got the money from television rights was long and bitter. Everyone realized that a lot of future money was at stake. At one stage it looked as though the actors would go on strike over the issue, but Ron continued with the tough negotiations and eventually won the day for SAG. The studios agreed that the actors would be entitled to a share of the profits—or a residual—every time a movie in which they acted was shown on television.

While Ron negotiated the details of the television rights agreement for SAG members, he managed to overlook a few important details in the contract of his next film. He had signed up to star in a movie titled *The Hasty Heart,* a war story set in Burma. The movie was about a crusty Scottish soldier who is dying, surrounded by international soldiers and a sympathetic nurse. Ron had assumed that he was signing up for the lead role, but he soon discovered that he was to play a supporting role. And worse, the movie was to be filmed in England.

The British government allowed American movies to be shown in Great Britain only if the profits from those screenings stayed in the country. This created a problem for the big movie studios. Because the studios had plenty of money in Great Britain that they had to spend there, they came up with the idea of making movies in Great Britain and using up the money in production costs. Ron did not want to leave the United States. If he was out of the country, how could he be an effective SAG president while the details of the television rights agreement were being worked out with the studios?

Because Jack Warner would not let Ron out of his contract, Ron took a train to the East Coast and sailed for England aboard the *Britannia* on November 2, 1948. Patricia Neal, the female star of the movie, and Vincent Sherman, the director, sailed with him. Ron was not looking forward to sailing across the Atlantic Ocean in winter.

Chapter 13

Nancy

Ron already knew that he disliked traveling by airplane, and he soon added ships to the list. His first crossing of the Atlantic Ocean was rough and wet as the *Britannia* sailed headlong into the worst storm in years. When he arrived at the Port of Southampton, Ron faced more weather records to endure. London was shrouded in the densest fog to engulf the city in a century. The buses crawled along the city streets as they were being guided through the fog by a conductor walking in front of the bus holding a flaming torch. And when Ron opened the hotel door, fog rolled into the lobby and hung there.

Everything about London in winter seemed gloomy. The sense of gloom was compounded by the fact that the city was still trying to rebuild after having been bombed heavily by the Germans during

World War II. Food rationing had ended, but it was still difficult to find a variety of food to buy, and electricity and gas consumption was closely regulated. No one was allowed to use electricity for frivolous things like lighting shop windows or displaying neon signs. Ron soon found that he had to keep feeding the gas heater in his hotel room with shilling coins or he would have no indoor heat.

Ron could not help but compare London to warm, lively Los Angeles. He soon had another comparison to make—the difference between a Hollywood movie studio and a London movie studio. *The Hasty Heart* was set in the steamy jungles of Burma, and all of the male actors in the film wore either pajamas or short pants with no shirts. The London studio did not want to spend money on heating, which meant that the inside of the studio was the same frigid temperature as outside. Ron spent many hours huddled in the corner trying to get warm between takes. Apart from the cold, the filming of the movie went well and even finished a little ahead of schedule.

This left Ron with eight days to fill before he had to sail back to the United States. Ron talked another actor into hiring a car and taking the ferry with him across the English Channel to France. He spent a wonderful week sightseeing. The only dark cloud on the trip was the amount of war damage still visible. Burned-out tanks and crashed fighter airplanes littered the countryside, and Ron and his friend had to take many detours around bombed-out bridges.

The voyage back across the Atlantic Ocean in February 1949 was more pleasant than the voyage out had been. Ron arrived back in Hollywood just in time for the Academy Awards. Jane Wyman had been nominated as best actress for her role in *Johnny Belinda,* and she won the best actress award. It was painful for Ron to watch her carrying her Oscar as she left the awards ceremony arm in arm with her new beau, her leading man in *Johnny Belinda.*

Ron's agent lined up some more movie roles for Ron as well as a few charity events. One of these events, the City of Hope Hospital's Charity Baseball Game, pitted male comedians against leading men in the movies. Ron never got past the first inning in the game. He was tripped sliding into first base, heard a snap, and then felt excruciating pain. He had broken his thighbone in three places.

Ron spent the next two months in traction, lying in a hospital bed thinking about the future and the past. He hoped that his leg would heal completely so he could get back to moviemaking sooner rather than later. In the meantime, he spent his days reading through SAG news and writing memos.

After two months in the hospital, Ron returned home to finish recuperating. Not long afterward, he received a phone call that would eventually change his life. The MGM director Mervyn LeRoy was at the other end of the line. He explained to Ron that a young actress named Nancy Davis was having trouble because she was being confused with another actress of the same name. It was against the SAG rules for two actresses to register with the guild using the same name, and LeRoy asked Ron if he would help Nancy resolve the issue.

Ron called Nancy and invited her to discuss her predicament with him over dinner. Nancy agreed to an early meal, and Ron wrote down her address so that he could pick her up.

Two hours later, Ron was standing at Nancy's front door in the Los Angeles suburb of Westwood. He felt a little self-conscious in doing so, as he still needed two canes to help him walk, but he straightened up as best he could as he rang the doorbell.

An auburn-haired young woman in a black-and-white dress promptly opened the door. She was shorter than most leading ladies in the movies, but it was her wide-set hazel eyes that Ron noticed first. Nancy's smile put Ron completely at ease as he introduced himself.

Soon Nancy and Ron were driving down the freeway toward La Rue, an upscale Hollywood restaurant, and chatting about the movies they were making. Ron was learning his lines for the upcoming movie *Storm Warning*, while Nancy had a small role as Helen Lee in *East Side, West Side.* Ron learned that Nancy had not been in Hollywood long. In fact, she was taking her screen test at the same time that Ron was returning from England by ship.

The conversation flowed freely at La Rue. Ron was surprised to learn that Nancy was the daughter of Edith Luckett, who had been an old-time Broadway actress. During her career, Nancy's mother had known many silent and modern movie stars, including Walter Huston, Jimmy Cagney, Spencer Tracy, and Katharine Hepburn. Nancy's adoptive father, Dr. Loyal Davis, was a leading neurosurgeon.

Even though Ron and Nancy had both insisted on the phone that they needed an early night, the two of them ended up visiting a nearby club. They watched the show twice, and Ron did not take Nancy home until two o'clock in the morning. The two had a great time together, and before he drove off, Ron promised that he would ask Nancy out again, only this time not to discuss business.

Soon Ron's broken leg had healed enough for him to begin work on his next movie, *Storm Warning,* which was being filmed in the small town of Corona, California. Ron still had to walk with a cane, but the director wrote the cane into the script.

Ron was on a roll again. After *Storm Warning* he was whisked off to Arizona to star in *The Last Outpost.* Best of all, he was allowed to bring along his own horse, Tar Baby, to ride in the filming of the movie.

Sometimes when he was back in Hollywood, Ron would call Nancy, and the two of them would go out together. Ron made it clear to Nancy, though, that he was not ready to settle down again. She agreed, and they both dated other people as well.

Two more movies followed, and then another, *Bedtime for Bonzo,* in which Ron had a special co-star— a chimpanzee named Bonzo. It did not take Ron long to realize that he was going to be upstaged by Bonzo. The chimp was a natural ham on camera.

Between his acting roles in movies, Ron became a popular speaker. On one occasion he was asked to give a speech before the Junior League convention in San Diego, 125 miles down the coast from

Hollywood. Ron was delighted to accept the invitation. He loved the drive down the Pacific Coast in his convertible. And when he thought about who he should ask to join him on the trip to San Diego, only one name came to mind—Nancy Davis.

Nancy agreed to go along, and the two of them set off. They had a wonderful time together and afterward decided that they would date only each other from then on. Many of their dates consisted of doing things around Ron's newly acquired house in Pacific Palisades or visiting their friends Bill and Ardis Holden. In fact, Bill Holden was the only man that Ron confided in when he decided to ask Nancy to marry him. Ron was delighted when Nancy accepted his proposal of marriage.

Ron did not want a big socialite wedding as his wedding to Jane Wyman had been. He and Nancy were married in a secret ceremony at the Little Brown Church in the Valley on March 4, 1952. Bill and Ardis Holden and the officiating minister were the only other people present. The press learned about the wedding while the couple were away honeymooning in Arizona, far from the glare of cameras. Ron and Nancy could not have been happier.

Many things in Ron's life changed after his marriage to Nancy Davis. The two of them discussed their career options. Nancy had spent the first six years of her life living with an aunt and uncle because her mother had insisted on pursuing a Broadway career and there was no way that she could take a child along with her. Because of this, Nancy had strong opinions about being a wife, mother, and career woman. "When it comes to a woman having a career and a family, something has to give," she said, making it clear to Ron that he would always come first. As a result, she asked to be released from her seven-year contract at the MGM studio.

Ron, too, was facing some big career decisions. He was now forty-one years old and was being offered middle-age roles, not the leading-man roles he had previously enjoyed. He knew that he did not want to watch his career take a slow, downward slide. Instead, he decided to wait and accept only really good offers.

Ron waited a year, but no worthwhile offer came his way. Meanwhile, Nancy was pregnant and then gave birth to a daughter on October 21, 1952, at Cedars of Lebanon Hospital. Ron and Nancy named their new daughter Patricia Ann Reagan.

Ron found it difficult to know what to do next. Within a year he had gone from being a carefree single man to having a wife and newborn child who depended on him. Ron had also gone from being the longest-serving president of the Screen Actors Guild to just being a board member. He had resigned as president of SAG on August 27, 1952, after spending six years in the position. He had decided that it was time for someone else to take over as president. Now Ron had to consider all his options.

He had received an offer to emcee an hour-long nightclub revue act at the Last Frontier Hotel in Las Vegas. For the first two weeks of the show, he would be paid as much as he was paid for a movie. It was a lot of money, and Ron decided to accept the offer.

Ron soon realized, however, that standing around in a smoky nightclub, cracking jokes and performing song and dance routines, was not really his scene. Although the reviews of the show were generally good, at the end of the two weeks he packed up and headed back to Hollywood, even though he was offered more work in Las Vegas.

Ron decided there had to be something better for him than emceeing Las Vegas shows. That something better came from an unexpected source. As a movie actor, Ron had always steered away from television. The conventional wisdom around Hollywood was that television work was the kiss of death to a serious actor, as it would lead to overexposure to the public.

Then two years after his marriage to Nancy, a man named Taft Schreiber told Ron that General Electric Company (GE) wanted to get into the television business. GE had asked for ideas as to what would appeal to the public. Taft had come up with the concept of a weekly show that would involve Ron's hosting a thirty-minute Sunday night program featuring a different condensed movie or dramatized story each week. Ron would be asked to act in several of the short dramas each season, but his main role on the show would be to introduce the dramas. Ron discussed the idea with Nancy. He had no doubt that it would be the end of his movie career, but would it be the beginning of something better? That was the question he had to wrestle with.

Chapter 14

Electric Living

Y ou can make your family's life much brighter
You will find your work much lighter
It's as easy as can be
When you live better e-lec-tric-ly
You can have your cake and you can eat it
Make life sweet it's hard to beat it
What a thrill to be so free
When you live better e-lec-tric-ly

So went the opening jingle for *General Electric Theater*. Ron took the job hosting the television show for $125,000 a year, and by 1954 he and Nancy *were* living better electrically!

It was obvious from the beginning that Ron was an ideal match for the show. Ron recruited most of the top stars in Hollywood to take the leading roles in the minidramas. He also talked about the latest innovations in electrical devices for the home and often interviewed top General Electric engineers. In one show he even imagined the day when a flat panel television set would be a reality. Ron's portions of the show were taped live, as were the commercials and many of the dramatic pieces. This made for some funny moments as the actors and advertising spokespeople ran from set to set.

Ron learned all that he could about General Electric, and he was impressed by what he discovered. The board of directors of GE had made a deliberate decision not to keep all of the company's factories and operational centers in one town or even one state. They believed that GE would be strongest if it decentralized and spread its manufacturing facilities over the entire United States. As a result, General Electric had 135 manufacturing plants employing over 700,000 workers spread around the United States.

For the most part, this strategy proved to be a good thing. Local conditions and labor disputes could not bring the company down. But the strategy also had a downside. The company needed to find a way to make all of its 700,000 employees around the country feel like they belonged to the larger GE family and feel connected to each other.

As host of *General Electric Theater,* Ron soon became the face of GE to the public, especially as his show became one of the ten most popular programs on television. The company decided to take advantage of Ron's popularity and send him on goodwill tours of GE plants all over the United States. Although Ron hated to be away from Nancy, this new opportunity excited him.

The first General Electric plant Ron visited was in Schenectady, New York. Ron had been told that the plant produced a wide range of appliances, from two-door refrigerator/freezers to the brand-new washer/drier combination unit. He had never been inside a manufacturing plant before, and the sheer size of this plant covering thirty acres was breathtaking. Ron stood on a metal balcony and looked over the factory floor below at a sea of machinists at work, tools, conveyer belts, hoists, and whirling motors.

Ron was escorted down onto the concrete factory floor, where he found the noise around him deafening, and his eyes stung as fumes settled on his contact lenses. As Ron walked around the factory floor, a machinist suddenly looked up and recognized him. He turned off his lathe, and Ron walked over to say hello. Then the man next to him switched off his machine, and soon a small group of workers had gathered around Ron. Some of them pulled pieces of paper from their pockets and asked Ron for his autograph. Others asked him about some of the leading ladies he had worked with in Hollywood or about other details of being a movie star. Ron cheerfully answered their questions and then moved on down the floor to where another group of workers had gathered.

Four hours passed before Ron found himself walking back up to the metal balcony that overlooked the factory floor. He was sure that he had talked to each worker in the plant, and he'd had a wonderful time doing so. Meeting blue-collar workers reminded him of his roots in Dixon, Illinois, where people made a living for themselves and their children by working hard.

Ron was scheduled to stay the night in Schenectady before going on to the next plant. Early that evening his host came to him with a strange request. About four thousand teachers were holding a convention in the town. Their keynote speaker for the evening had become ill and was unable to speak to the group, who now needed a replacement speaker. Since everyone knew who Ronald Reagan was, the host asked Ron if he would speak to the group.

At first Ron was surprised. He didn't have time to do any research and write a speech. Then he thought about all the political and social commentary books he had read over the years that discussed the state of education in the country. Before he knew it, he was standing in front of the group listening to himself say that he was glad to be speaking to the group.

Ron's speech was a huge hit. The teachers gave Ron a ten-minute standing ovation. Ron left the meeting glad that he had agreed to speak. He had learned something valuable about himself in the process—all of the knowledge that he had absorbed over the years was waiting inside him for a chance to come out. He felt invigorated to think that he was able to reach out to others with his beliefs and connect with them.

As the years rolled by, Ron found himself speaking to many more groups: the American Legion, Lions, the Elks, Rotary, and the Kiwanis. Sometimes the group picked the topic they wanted him to speak on, and sometimes Ron chose it and found himself giving his views on everything from the country's economic woes to juvenile delinquency.

As he listened to himself speak, an interesting thing happened. Ron had to face the fact that he sounded a lot more like a Republican than a Democrat. Somewhere along the way, things had changed. He often later said, "I did not desert the Democratic Party; it deserted me." By this he meant that even though he was still a registered Democrat, he felt the party no longer represented his interests and, by extension, the interests of the country as a whole. He found that Republican values were more to his taste. Ron had to admit that this was a big change for someone who had loyally supported Franklin Roosevelt throughout his years as president.

Back home in California, Ron and Nancy were building a new house for themselves at 1669 San Onofre Drive in Pacific Palisades. Nestled on the southern slope of the Santa Monica Mountains, the house had an unobstructed, sweeping view of Los Angeles and the Pacific Ocean. Ron and Nancy had the architect design the place so that most of the rooms took advantage of the view.

Ron joked that the new house had every electrical appliance and gadget available, except the electric chair. This was not quite accurate: the house actually had several appliances that were not yet available to the general public. These appliances, which were gifts from General Electric, included a dishwasher with a built-in garbage disposal, a retractable roof for indoor/outdoor dining, and a film projection room. Nancy selected all of the furnishings for the house, and the place looked stunning with gray carpets and black furniture. Ron and Nancy both agreed that red was their favorite color, and they used red accents throughout the house.

When the house was complete, Ron and Nancy loved it and the beauty of the hills around them. They enjoyed each other's company in relative seclusion, and the press dubbed them The Golden Couple.

Even though Ron had thought that taking the GE hosting job on television would mean the end of his movie career, he was wrong. Attitudes in Hollywood were changing, and television was becoming an integral part of most Americans' lives. And so in 1957 Ron was offered a role in a movie. He read the script for *Hellcats of the Navy* and liked what he read. He was asked to play the part of Casey Abbott, a submarine commander sent on dangerous missions into Japanese-controlled waters. His love interest was Helen Blair, a nurse aboard the submarine. The movie's director suggested that Nancy might like to play the part of Helen Blair.

Ron and Nancy signed on for *Hellcats of the Navy*. It was the first and only movie they made together, but they enjoyed the experience on the set.

Ron had not calculated just how difficult it would be for him to be cramped up in a submarine during filming. He was claustrophobic and could hardly wait for the filming to end. And Nancy couldn't wait for it to be over as well, but for a different reason. During the filming of the movie she learned that she was pregnant again.

When it opened in movie theaters, *Hellcats of the Navy* did not get good reviews, and Ron threw himself even more into his job hosting *General Electric Theater.* But deep down he worried about what he would do if that job ever came to an end.

On May 20, 1958, Nancy gave birth to a son, whom they named Ronald Prescott Reagan. Patricia, or Patti, as she was called, was now five and a half years old, and Ron's two older children, Maureen and Michael, were seventeen and thirteen, respectively. Ron had tried to stay in touch with Maureen and Michael as best he could, but inevitably they had drifted apart. Ron's work, his traveling, and his new family with Nancy kept him busy enough for two men.

As he always did, Ron made the time to follow politics. As 1960 rolled around, the two U.S. political parties began the process of selecting candidates to run in the presidential election in November. Even though Dwight Eisenhower was a popular president, the twenty-second amendment precluded him from running for a third term as president. In the end, the Republicans chose Vice President Richard Nixon as their candidate for president, and the Democrats settled on John F. Kennedy, the forty-three-year-old senator from Massachusetts.

Ron watched the political conventions with interest. Even though he was still a registered Democrat, he had voted for and supported Eisenhower. And now as the election approached, he once again decided to throw his support behind the Republican candidate. He declared himself to be a Democrat for Nixon. The election was close, but Kennedy won and was sworn into office as thirty-fifth President of the United States on January 20, 1961.

Other things were changing in America. *General Electric Theater* was becoming dated. New drama shows were taking hold of the popular imagination. A new Western drama series called *Bonanza* was now drawing more viewers than *General Electric Theater,* and in May 1962 the last episode of the show was filmed.

General Electric Theater had enjoyed a great run. Ron had hosted two hundred episodes in the nearly nine years the show had been on the air. Also, traveling the country and talking personally with over a quarter of a million people had sharpened Ron's political views and honed his speech-making and other communication skills. He had gained confidence, authority, and fame. Now he just had to figure out what he wanted to do with these skills.

One thing he did do in 1962 was to officially switch from being a Democrat to becoming a member of the Republican Party. After all, Ron had been supporting Republican candidates ever since Dwight Eisenhower was in office.

Ron was still considering his options as to what to do when his mother died on July 25, 1962. Nelle had been living in a nursing home for some time, suffering from dementia. Her long, slow decline had been painful for Ron to witness. Now that she was gone, he felt sad. It was difficult to adjust to the death of his mother. Although Neil (Moon) Reagan lived nearby, the two brothers were not particularly close. Ron realized that his family ties were now stronger with Nancy's family, especially her father, than with anyone else.

Ron continued to take an active interest in national politics. He kept up with what was happening in South Vietnam. Since 1959, the United States had been quietly sending military advisors and special forces troops to the country to help the South Vietnamese fight off the Communist North Vietnamese, who were trying to take over the country, in what many saw as the menacing advance of Communism throughout the world. Nearly sixteen thousand American forces and advisors were now serving in Vietnam. Like many people, Ron believed that the United States had to take a strong stand against Communism around the world.

On November 22, 1963, American politics took an ugly turn. President John F. Kennedy was assassinated in Dallas, Texas. Vice President Lyndon Johnson was quickly sworn into office to replace John F. Kennedy and in the process inherited many global problems, including the Vietnam War.

The following year, 1964, the Vietnam War became an issue in the presidential election. President Johnson was running for office on a peace platform, while the Republican candidate, Senator Barry Goldwater, argued that the use of nuclear weapons might be necessary to win the war against Communism.

Ron knew Senator Goldwater personally. Goldwater was a neighbor of Nancy's parents in Arizona, and the two families were good friends. Ron backed Goldwater's stand and offered to do whatever he could to help the senator get elected President.

The election campaign became very emotional, with Lyndon Johnson and his followers accusing Goldwater and the Republicans of wanting to ignite a nuclear war. The Republicans responded by accusing Johnson and the Democrats of being soft on Communism and unwilling to halt its dangerous spread across Asia.

Neither party seemed to have a clear majority, and things grew tense as the election approached. One day in October, Ron received a phone call from Barry Goldwater asking him to make a nationally televised speech in support of the senator's bid for the presidency.

Ron agreed and got out his old speeches from his General Electric days to reread. He knew the stakes were high, but he also knew that he could come up with a speech that would connect with the American people. He titled his speech "A Time for Choosing."

On the evening of October 27, 1964, millions of Americans switched on their television sets to watch Ronald Reagan deliver his speech on the CBS network. Ron had given the speech before a live audience several days before, and the speech had been taped for replay on television. Ron began slowly and deliberately.

Thank you. Thank you very much. Thank you, and good evening. The sponsor has been identified, but unlike most television programs, the performer hasn't been provided with a script. As a matter of fact, I have been permitted to choose my own words and discuss my own ideas regarding the choice that we face in the next few weeks. I have spent most of my life as a Democrat. I recently have seen fit to follow another course. I believe that the issues confronting us cross party lines. Now, one side in this campaign has been telling us that the issues of this election are the maintenance of peace and prosperity. The line has been used, "We've never had it so good."

But I have an uncomfortable feeling that this prosperity isn't something on which we can base our hopes for the future. No nation in history has ever survived a tax burden that reached a third of its national income. Today, 37 cents out of every dollar earned in this country is the tax collector's share, and yet our government continues to spend 17 million dollars a day more than the government takes in. We haven't balanced our budget 28 out of the last 34 years. We've raised our debt limit three times in the last twelve months, and now our national debt is one and a half times bigger than all the combined debts of all the nations of the world. We have 15 billion dollars in gold in our treasury; we don't own an ounce. Foreign dollar claims are 27.3

billion dollars. And we've just had announced that the dollar of 1939 will now purchase 45 cents in its total value.

Every so often Ron scanned the crowd before him to make sure that they were still with him. They were. Twenty-seven minutes after beginning his speech, he concluded with the following words:

You and I know and do not believe that life is so dear and peace so sweet as to be pur-chased at the price of chains and slavery. If nothing in life is worth dying for, when did this begin—just in the face of this enemy? Or should Moses have told the children of Israel to live in slavery under the pharaohs? Should Christ have refused the cross? Should the patriots at Concord Bridge have thrown down their guns and refused to fire the shot heard 'round the world? The martyrs of history were not fools, and our honored dead who gave their lives to stop the advance of the Nazis didn't die in vain. Where, then, is the road to peace? Well, it's a simple answer after all. You and I have the courage to say to our enemies, "There is a price we will not pay. There is a point beyond which they must not advance." And this—this is the meaning in the phrase of Barry Goldwater's "peace through strength." Winston Churchill said, "The destiny of man is not measured by material computations. When great forces are on the move in the

world, we learn we're spirits—not animals."
And he said, "There's something going on in
time and space, and beyond time and space,
which, whether we like it or not, spells duty."

You and I have a rendezvous with destiny.
We'll preserve for our children this, the last
best hope of man on earth, or we'll sentence
them to take the last step into a thousand
years of darkness.

We will keep in mind and remember that
Barry Goldwater has faith in us. He has faith
that you and I have the ability and the dignity
and the right to make our own decisions and
determine our own destiny.

As it turned out, it was Ronald Reagan who had a
rendezvous with destiny. His speech was not enough
to get Barry Goldwater elected, and Lyndon Johnson
won the election for the Democrats. But the United
States had seen in Ron a man they liked better than
Barry Goldwater. Republicans began asking themselves whether they could have won the election had
Ronald Reagan been their nominee. In the speech
Ron was confident, charismatic, and informed—the
very qualities a strong president needed.

On November 5, 1964, the day after Lyndon
Johnson won the election, a group of conservative
Republicans got together and formed a group, which
they called Republicans for Ronald Reagan.

Chapter 15

Governor

On January 4, 1966, Ronald Reagan looked straight into the television camera and delivered some of the most important lines of his life. "Today, I say to the people of California, I announce my intention to seek the Republican nomination for governor."

It was a calculated move. While riding the wave of public enthusiasm generated by his televised "A Time for Choosing" speech, Ron had been urged to work toward the presidency of the United States. Other advisors, however, suggested that he make a run for a lesser office first and work his way up to a bid to become president. Ron agreed with the advice of these advisors, and thus began his campaign to become the next governor of California.

On June 2, 1966, Ron easily won the Republican Party's nomination as its candidate for governor.

Thanks to all of his years speaking to audiences on behalf of General Electric and his experience in the movies, Ron was at ease speaking to both large crowds and small groups.

Now that he was the Republican candidate for governor, Ron knew that he had to set an example for the young people of the state. When he had taken up smoking in Des Moines, people did not know that it was a dangerous habit. Now things had changed. Links were being made between smoking and cancer. Ron decided that it was time for him to give up smoking. But he needed something to distract him, so he took up eating jelly beans.

Ron ate a lot of jelly beans as he contemplated the challenge ahead of him. The current governor, Democrat Pat Brown, was a well-liked public figure who had brought many positive changes to California in his eight years in office. Everyone agreed that the construction of eight new state university campuses, more than one thousand miles of new freeways, and a better aqueduct system to bring fresh water to the cities were good things for California.

Republicans and Democrats argued, however, about other issues. Governor Brown championed state government becoming more involved in creating and funding social welfare programs, including more hospitals and mental health institutions, and in writing new civil rights laws.

Ron carefully studied the governor's stance on all of these issues and prepared to confront him on them. He believed strongly that all levels of government should have as little intrusion into people's lives as possible. Churches and other such civic-minded groups should help the poor and the needy. He believed that the government's job was to protect jobs and allow free enterprise to create more of them so that everyone could pay his or her own way in society rather than wait for the government to hand out money. This was the standard ideological division between Democrats and Republicans.

As Ron campaigned, he watched the nightly news on television and the commercials between news programs. As he did so, it became obvious to him the tactics that Pat Brown and his campaign were using to discredit him. Over and over, Ron heard Brown say things like, "I am a politician. You wouldn't go to a movie to watch me play the leading man. Why would you vote for an actor to lead our great state?"

Sometimes Governor Brown would remind Californians that while he was improving their state, Ronald Reagan was costarring in a movie with Bonzo the chimpanzee. Things began to turn ugly as the campaigning went on.

Next, Senator Edward Kennedy came to California to help in Pat Brown's campaign. Senator Kennedy was a young, vigorous man with movie-star looks himself, who had come from a wealthy, political family. He told those who came to hear him speak, "Reagan has never held any political office, and here he is seeking the top spot in the government of California."

In his next speech, Ron fought back. "I understand," he said, "there's a senator from Massachusetts who's come to California and he's concerned that I've never held office prior to seeking this job. Well, you know, come to think of it, the senator from Massachusetts never held *any* job before he became a senator."

The campaign was like a boxing match, and Pat Brown threw the next punch, saying, "Reagan is only an actor who memorizes speeches written by other people, just like he memorized the lines that were fed to him by his screenwriters in the movies. Sure, he makes a good speech, but who's *writing* his speeches?"

Ron was incensed by this allegation. He always wrote his own speeches. However, he knew that it would not sound convincing if he were to get up and tell people this. They might think that someone wrote those lines for him to say as well. Ron had to find a better way to show the people of California that he was not a puppet of rich Republicans in the state.

Ron discussed the matter with Nancy and his advisors to come up with a solution. "I'll have to get away from reading my speeches completely," Ron told his team. "From now on, I'm only going to speak to a group for a few minutes, and then I am going to open it up for questions. I'll take questions on anything and do my best to answer them honestly. That way people will see I am not following a script."

This was a bold move, since there were many areas of government that Ron knew little about. To help him overcome this problem, his advisors told him to be willing to look people in the eye and tell them straight out that he did not yet completely understand an issue and so was not ready to give an answer or, more directly, to just say, "I don't know." This was a departure from the approach of most political figures, who had an opinion on everything, but Ron found it worked well for him. By taking this approach, he came across as humble and ready to learn more before making pronouncements.

As election day drew closer, the Brown campaign began to get alarmed. Ron smiled. He knew that if the Brown campaign was becoming scared of losing the election, they might well use poor judgment in their campaigning. And they did. Pat Brown appeared in a television commercial talking to a group of school-children. In the commercial, the governor told the children, "I'm running against an actor, and you know who killed Abe Lincoln, don't you?"

Ron's campaign grew angry at this slight. Pat Brown had compared Ronald Reagan to John Wilkes Booth, the actor who assassinated Abraham Lincoln, one of the United States' most beloved presidents. But Ron just smiled to himself. He knew that Governor Brown had gone too far and that the people of California would see through his tactics.

Ron was right. On Election Day, November 8, 1966, Governor Pat Brown received 2.7 million votes, and Ronald Reagan received 3.7 million votes. The victory was a landslide for a Republican in a traditionally Democratic state.

On January 3, 1967, Ron was sworn into office as the thirty-third governor of California. Maureen Reagan, who would celebrate her twenty-sixth birthday the next day, and twenty-one-year-old Michael Reagan stood proudly beside their father. Maureen now worked as a political planner, while Michael was a used boat salesman. Ron and Nancy moved into the governor's mansion in Sacramento. Ron Jr. was now nearly nine years old. Patti was fourteen and had come home from boarding school for the event.

In his inaugural speech as governor, Ron said, "For many years now, you and I have been shushed like children and told there are no simple answers to the complex problems which are beyond our comprehension. Well, the truth is that there are simple answers—there are just no easy ones."

Ron was referring to the problems the state government had encountered in keeping its spending within the budget. Ron promised that he would not raise taxes but would cut spending until the amount the government brought in was equal to the amount it spent.

This proved more difficult to do than Ron had imagined it would be. He soon discovered that California was $194 million in debt. He immediately ordered state agencies to cut their spending by ten percent, and he instituted a freeze on new hiring. But cost cutting alone was not enough to get the state out of its precarious financial situation. In the end, and very reluctantly, Ron had to do the opposite of what he had promised. Instead of cutting taxes, he was forced to raise them. Corporate, personal, and sales tax rates went up, though Ron did manage to lower property taxes.

In 1968 some key players within the Republican Party came to Ron and asked him to put his name in as a candidate for the nomination to run for the office of President of the United States. The group explained that they did not think he would win the nomination, but they needed Ron to help split the vote between Richard Nixon, Nelson Rockefeller, and George Romney. In the 1964 bid for the Republican nomination, a lot of bitter feelings had arisen. The group felt that by adding Ron to the mix they would have a more even balance of conservative and liberal Republicans.

Ron was not eager to join a race that he knew he would lose and one that would take him away from his new job as governor, but he could see the logic of the group's argument. He agreed to the plan, and as expected, he lost the nomination to Richard Nixon. Following Richard Nixon's nomination, Ron turned his attention back to California. The state still had plenty of problems that needed to be solved.

One of the problems that Ron focused on was what to do about the state of civil disorder that existed on many university campuses across California. During 1967 the number of young men being drafted to serve in Vietnam had increased. This in turn led to demonstrations about the war. These demonstrations had been mostly peaceful affairs, but during 1968 the protests had grown bigger and more violent as protestors and police clashed in cities across the United States.

A radicalized free speech movement had also grown up on college campuses around California and particularly on the University of California campus at Berkeley. There was also increased agitation for greater civil rights and women's rights. By 1969

Ron felt that a state of anarchy was beginning to set in on the campus at Berkeley. And when Cal students seized a piece of university land to make into a park, Ron decided he had to act to restore order. He declared, "This administration will do whatever is possible to maintain order on our campuses.... I don't care what force it takes. That force must be applied."

That is what he did. Ron ordered National Guardsmen and state troopers onto the University of California campus in Berkeley to stop the protests and restore order.

All of these decisions could have weighed heavily on Ron as governor, but Ron was determined to keep a balance in his life and not wear himself out. He worked five days a week and then went home. He often went for a swim and ate a simple meal before retiring to his room to watch a television program or two.

On the weekends, the Reagans normally returned to their Pacific Palisades home or to the ranch Ron and Nancy had bought near Malibu. Ron loved it at the ranch. He could ride horses, mend fences, and dig ditches—hard labor in the golden California sun.

In 1970 Ron was easily elected to a second term as governor. This time he had the experience needed to tackle the welfare problem head-on. Harking back to his days with the Screen Actors Guild, he knew that he had to work across party lines to accomplish his goal. He formed an alliance with the leading Democrat, Bob Moretti. Together the two of them brainstormed and came up with the California Welfare Reform Act. The aim of the act was to support those who truly needed help and weed out those who did not. The act was passed into law, and it worked well. The number of people on the state's welfare rolls dropped by 330,000, saving California two billion dollars, while payments to those who could prove they were in real need rose by fifty percent. Ron was pleased with the outcome.

By the end of his second term as governor in 1975, Ron's administration had given the people of California four tax rebates and the government was running smoothly. California was no longer known as the welfare capital of America.

After two terms as governor, Ron felt that his work was done. He was sixty-five years old. Although many people wanted him to run for a third term, he decided not to. It was time for a change. That change came in the form of a ranch named Rancho del Cielo (Ranch in the Sky). The ranch was a 688-acre parcel of land located atop the Santa Ynez mountain range northwest of Santa Barbara, California.

From the first time Ron set foot on the property, he fell in love with the place and quickly bought it. An adobe house sat beside a small lake on the ranch, and the view from the house looked out across the lake and an expansive meadow, with trees and mountains beyond. From several points on the property Ron could look out and see boats plying the Santa Barbara channel. Ron and Nancy made some alterations to the house and moved in. Ron loved nothing better at the ranch than to ride his horse and enjoy the serenity and beauty of the location. It was such a change from the busy life he had lived as governor in Sacramento.

Even at Rancho del Cielo, politics intruded into Ron and Nancy's life. The Republican Party was in shambles. On August 9, 1974, Richard Nixon had been forced to resign from the presidency as a result of the Watergate scandal. And in April 1975, the North Vietnamese captured Saigon, the capital of South Vietnam. The United States had lost the Vietnam War. As a result, only eighteen percent of Americans identified themselves as Republicans.

Vice President Gerald Ford had been sworn in as president upon Nixon's resignation, but the public seemed to view the new president as a nice but weak man. What America needed more than ever was a strong, forthright, honest leader. Many within the Republican Party felt that Ronald Reagan, the popular former governor of a large and progressive state, was their best hope in the presidential election coming up in 1976. Members of the party barraged Ron with letters and phone calls until he agreed to run against Gerald Ford to be the Republican nominee for president.

Ron campaigned hard against the sitting president for the nomination. At the Republican Convention in Kansas City in August 1976, the result was close, with Gerald Ford receiving 117 more delegate votes than Ron. Even though he had lost his bid to be the Republican nominee, Ron threw his weight behind Gerald Ford's candidacy and campaigned for him in over twenty states. At the election on

November 2, 1976, however, public support swung the way of Jimmy Carter, the Democratic nominee, who was sworn in as the thirty-ninth president of the United States on January 20, 1977.

With the United States firmly back in the hands of the Democrats, Ron knew that he had his work cut out for him. Despite the uphill battle, he was determined to become the next president of the United States. He had slightly less than four years in which to campaign before the next presidential election in November 1980, and he had a lot of work to do in that time.

Chapter 16

The Will of the People

On July 17, 1980, Ronald Reagan stood alone on the platform at the Republican Convention in Detroit, Michigan. The slogan beneath the podium read "Together...A New Beginning." And it was a new beginning for Ron and Nancy. After three years of tireless campaigning around the country, Ron had won the Republican nomination for president. As flags waved and the crowd chanted, "We want Ronnie!" Ron spoke.

> More than anything else, I want my candidacy to unify our country; to renew the American spirit and sense of purpose. I want to carry our message to every American, regardless of party affiliation, who is a member of this community of shared values.

Never before in our history have Americans been called upon to face three grave threats to our very existence, any one of which could destroy us. We face a disintegrating economy, a weakened defense, and an energy policy based on the sharing of scarcity.

The major issue of this campaign is the direct political, personal, and moral responsibility of Democratic Party leadership—in the White House and in Congress—for this unprecedented calamity which has befallen us. They tell us they have done the most that humanly could be done. They say that the United States has had its day in the sun, that our nation has passed its zenith. They expect you to tell your children that the American people no longer have the will to cope with their problems, that the future will be one of sacrifice and few opportunities.

My fellow citizens, I utterly reject that view. The American people, the most generous on earth, who created the highest standard of living, are not going to accept the notion that we can only make a better world for others by moving backwards ourselves. Those who believe we can have no business leading the nation.

I will not stand by and watch this great country destroy itself under mediocre leadership that drifts from one crisis to the next, eroding our national will and purpose. We have come together here because the American people deserve better from those to whom they entrust our nation's highest offices, and we stand united in our resolve to do something about it.

We need rebirth of the American tradition of leadership at every level of government and in private life as well. The United States of America is unique in world history because it has a genius for leaders—many leaders—on many levels. But back in 1976, Mr. Carter said, "Trust me." And a lot of people did. Now, many of those people are out of work. Many have seen their savings eaten away by inflation. Many others on fixed incomes, especially the elderly, have watched helplessly as the cruel tax of inflation wasted away their purchasing power. And, today, a great many who trusted Mr. Carter wonder if we can survive the Carter policies of national defense.

"Trust me" government asks that we concentrate our hopes and dreams on one man, that we trust him to do what's best for us. My view of government places trust not in one person or one party but in those values that transcend persons and parties. The trust is where it belongs—in the people. The responsibility to live up to that trust is where it belongs, in their elected leaders....

Tonight, let us dedicate ourselves to renewing the American compact. I ask you not simply to trust me but to trust your values—our values—and to hold me responsible for living up to them. I ask you to trust that American spirit which knows no ethnic, religious, social, political, regional, or economic boundaries, the spirit that burned with zeal in the hearts of millions of immigrants from every corner of the earth who came here in search of freedom.

Some say that spirit no longer exists. But I have seen it—I have felt it—all across the land, in the big cities, the small towns, and in rural America. The American spirit is still there, ready to blaze into life if you and I are willing to do what has to be done, the practical, down-to-earth things that will stimulate our economy, increase productivity, and put America back to work.

The time is now to resolve that the basis of a firm and principled foreign policy is one that takes the world as it is and seeks to change it by leadership and example, not by harangue, harassment, or wishful thinking.

The time is now to say that while we shall seek new friendships and expand and improve others, we shall not do so by breaking our word or casting aside old friends and allies.

And, the time is now to redeem promises once made to the American people by another candidate, in another time and another place. He said, "For three long years I have been going up and down this country preaching that government—federal, state, and local—costs too much. I shall not stop that preaching. As an immediate program of action, we must abolish useless offices. We must eliminate unnecessary functions of government...we must consolidate subdivisions of government and, like the private citizen, give up luxuries which we can no longer afford.

"I propose to you, my friends, and through you that government of all kinds, big and little, be made solvent and that the example be set by the President of the United States and his Cabinet."

So said Franklin Delano Roosevelt in his acceptance speech to the Democratic National Convention in July 1932.

The time is now, my fellow Americans, to recapture our destiny, to take it into our own hands. But to do this will take many of us, working together. I ask you tonight to volunteer your help in this cause so we can carry our message throughout the land.

Yes, isn't now the time that we, the people, carried out these unkept promises? Let us pledge to each other and to all America on this July day forty-eight years later, we intend to do just that.

Ron stopped for a moment. He felt tears welling up within and a lump forming in his throat. Then he went on.

I have thought of something that is not part of my speech, and I'm worried over whether I should do it.

Can we doubt that only a Divine Providence placed this land, this island of freedom, here as a refuge for all those people in the world who yearn to breathe freely: Jews and Christians enduring persecution behind the Iron Curtain, the boat people of Southeast Asia, of Cuba and Haiti, the victims of drought and famine in Africa, the freedom fighters of Afghanistan, and our own countrymen held in savage captivity.

I'll confess that I've been a little afraid to suggest what I'm going to suggest—I'm more afraid not to—that we begin our crusade joined together in a moment of silent prayer.

Ron bowed his head, and the crowd joined him in silent prayer. A moment later he concluded, "God Bless America." Then George H. W. Bush, Ron's choice for vice president, joined him on the stage. Ron beckoned for Nancy to join him at the podium as well. Beaming, Nancy came over, held Ron's hand, and waved to the cheering crowd with him.

Yet as the crowd cheered, Ron knew that they had a long way to go. Four months of hard campaigning lay ahead. But with George Bush and Nancy at his side, Ron felt optimistic about the future. Americans needed hope and pride again, and he believed that he was the man to give it to them.

It was five-thirty in the afternoon on Election Day, November 4, 1980. Ron was in the shower thinking about his plans for the evening. He and Nancy were off to a friend's house to watch the election results come in. The first results to be announced would be from the East Coast, where, since it was three hours ahead of California, the polls had already closed. Then around nine o'clock, an hour after the polls closed in California and the results from the West Coast had started rolling in, Ron and Nancy would go to the Republican Party campaign headquarters to await the final tally and the news of whether or not he would be the next president of the United States.

Standing in the shower contemplating the evening ahead, Ron heard Nancy's voice breaking into his thoughts. "Ron, you need to get out of the shower and come to the phone."

Ron poked his head out, puzzled as to what phone call could be so urgent that it could not wait until he had finished showering.

"It's Jimmy Carter!" Nancy exclaimed.

Ron turned off the water, wrapped a towel around himself, and hurried over to the telephone. "Yes, Mr. President," he said.

"Governor Reagan, allow me to be the first to congratulate you," came the voice of Jimmy Carter.

Ron felt his whole body relax as a broad smile swept over his face. He gave Nancy a thumbs-up. Even before all the polls across the country had closed, the will of the people was evident. The people wanted Ronald Reagan as fortieth president of the United States.

When he hung up the telephone, Ron engulfed Nancy in a hug.

Later that night the final results were announced. Ronald Reagan had won 43,899,248 votes, while Jimmy Carter had won 35,481,435. It was a clear victory for Ron and the Republican Party. The next day the national news headlines ran the gamut from "The Gipper Takes the Big One" to "There Will Be Jelly Beans in the White House!"

Two and a half months later, just before noon on January 20, 1981, Ronald Wilson Reagan was sworn in as president of the United States. At sixty-nine years of age, he was the oldest man ever to be sworn in to the office. It was an unseasonably warm fifty-five degrees in Washington, D.C., that day. Ron felt quite warm in his morning coat. As he took the oath of office, he placed his hand on the old Bible that his mother had read to him as a boy.

When the swearing-in ceremony was over and he had given his inaugural address to the crowd gathered on the mall to witness the occasion, Ron stepped into a room in the Capitol where he performed his first act as president. He signed an executive order removing price controls on gasoline and oil, eliminating government control in that industry. He wanted to show the world that he meant business about reducing government involvement in the private sector.

After the official inaugural lunch in the National Statuary Hall in the Capitol, Ron and Nancy proceeded to the viewing stand outside the White House to watch the inaugural parade come down

Pennsylvania Avenue, just as it had since Thomas
Jefferson was sworn in as president in 1805. Near
the front of the parade was the Dixon High School
band. Ron laughed with delight when he saw their
purple uniforms come into view. For a moment he
was Dutch Reagan again, back at Lowell Park, scan-
ning the water of the Rock River, ready to dive in to
save someone in need.

As the band marched past, Ron looked at the
young band members and tried to imagine the thrill
it would have been for him when he was a high school
student if he had come all the way to Washington,
D.C., to see an alumnus become president. "Yes,"
Ron said to himself, "America is a land of great hope
and promise. If I, a poor kid from Dixon, Illinois, can
make it to the White House, anyone can!"

Later that night Ron and Nancy made the rounds
of the inaugural balls being held in Washington and
danced together at all eight of them. It was one of
the happiest nights of Ron's life. Ron could scarcely
believe it—he was president of the United States of
America, and his leading lady, Nancy, was the first
lady of the land.

Chapter 17

A Survivor

R on soon found that life, even in the White House, took on a surprisingly normal routine. Many times he felt like he was a governor again, just of a larger state. His routine started the first day in office. He had breakfast upstairs in the White House with Nancy. Breakfast consisted of his usual fare: fruit juice, bran cereal, and decaffeinated coffee. As he ate, he skimmed through *The Washington Post* newspaper, taking time to read the comics pages, and then looked over *The New York Times*. At nine o'clock he took the elevator down to the Oval Office, where his schedule for the day was waiting on his desk. Next to the schedule were the papers and notes that needed Ron's attention.

After having lunch upstairs with Nancy, Ron went back to his office to continue with meetings and talks. At six o'clock Ron's day was officially over, though he did read important papers at night.

On February 5, 1981, just over two weeks into his presidency, Ron made his first televised speech to the nation from the Oval Office. Using an array of charts and graphs, he explained that the country was in financial trouble. Interest rates were approaching twenty percent, inflation was rampant, and unemployment rates were sky-high.

After delivering the discouraging news Ron looked directly into the camera and said, "In this present crisis, government is not the solution to our problems; government is the problem." He went on to say, "It's time to try something different, and that's what we're going to do." Ron explained that he was going to start by instituting income tax cuts for everyone at a rate of ten percent a year for three years and that he was going to take the burden off rich people, who paid proportionally higher taxes than poor people. He pointed out that it was rich people who created opportunities for poor people to be employed and that they needed to be encouraged to spend their money on creating more jobs rather than give it to the government in the form of taxes.

Ron outlined other steps that needed to be taken immediately. Federal spending had to be cut. Government regulations must be examined, and those that were too meddling needed to be removed. And the government had to figure out a way to move toward balancing the budget.

Two days later, Ron celebrated his seventieth birthday. He had never felt better or happier.

Despite the challenges that came with the job, he was thrilled to be president. In the limousine on the way to the inauguration, President Carter had described the presidency as a burden, but Ron did not feel burdened at all. He was certain that this was the best chance he'd ever have to use his ideas and time to make a real difference in the country and in the world.

Ron was also determined not to get bogged down in the minute details of the presidency. He felt that he had picked a competent staff and that his role was to inspire them, make sure that they were clear as to his wishes, and then leave them to figure out how to get the job done.

Of course, many people did not agree with Ron's ideas or actions. Ron had said that he would rein in government spending. He did so by cutting eighty-three major government-funded programs, upsetting more than a few people. Despite the reaction of people to his decisions, rather than hide inside the White House, Ron used every opportunity available to get out among the people and sell his ideas.

On March 30, 1981, Ron found himself speaking at a luncheon meeting of the Building Construction Trades Conference at the Washington Hilton Hotel in Washington, D.C. The group was not a particularly friendly crowd, but Ron did not mind speaking to them. He warmed them up with a couple of jokes to start and took questions at the end of his speech.

When the meeting was over, Ron exited the hotel by a side door to a waiting limousine. Surrounded by his contingent of Secret Service agents, he walked out onto T Street. A small crowd cheered as he emerged from the hotel. As he slowed down to wave to them, he heard a strange sound, six loud pops in quick succession.

"What's that?" Ron said, turning to Agent Jerry Parr. Much to Ron's astonishment Jerry tackled him. Just as Ron was about to go down, another agent rushed over and pushed both Ron and Jerry into the back of the limousine. Ron could hear shouts of "Get him out! Get him out!" as he hit the floor of the limousine. The door quickly slammed shut behind him.

"Take off!" Jerry yelled, and the limousine sped away.

An excruciating pain shot down Ron's left side. "Get off me, Jerry," Ron said. "I think you've broken one of my ribs."

The two men disentangled from each other and climbed onto the back seat of the limousine. Jerry ran his hands down Ron's back and side. "No blood," he said.

Suddenly, as if on cue, Ron coughed, and bright red blood frothed out of his mouth. Ron wiped the blood away with his handkerchief. "I think I've cut my mouth as well," he said.

Jerry took one look at the president and yelled to the driver, "Get us to GW!"

The limousine swerved into a side street and roared off toward George Washington University Hospital five blocks away.

Ron struggled to understand what was happening. He tried to take a breath—a shallow breath so as not to jar his ribcage—but he could not get air into his lungs. He sat up straight and tried again. "I can't breathe," he gasped as a wave of panic swept over him.

The limousine screeched to a halt outside the emergency room. Jerry opened the car door and said, "I'll get a gurney."

"No," Ron replied, "I'll walk in." With that, he swung his legs around, stood up, and leaned on Jerry's arm. Together they walked the twenty feet to the emergency room entrance. The automatic doors swung open just as Ron collapsed onto one knee.

Ron was aware of being lifted onto a gurney, and it seemed to him like people were all around him. Someone was cutting his suit off him, and then he saw the gleam of a knife at his throat. Ron closed his eyes as the knife made a small cut and a breathing tube was pushed into his throat. Then he lost consciousness.

A few minutes later Ron regained consciousness. Then Ron saw Nancy walking toward him, a jar of jelly beans in her hand. Ron tried to smile, but he couldn't manage it. Instead, as Nancy bent over him he tried humor. "Honey, I forgot to duck," he said, borrowing the line that boxer Jack Dempsey had told his wife the night he was defeated by Gene Tunney. Nancy did not laugh at his joke.

After more prodding and probing of Ron's body, a doctor leaned over to talk to Ron. "Mr. President, sir, we need to operate. Do we have your permission?"

"Yes, and please tell me you are a Republican," Ron quipped.

"We all are Republicans here today, sir," the doctor said.

Just then a gurney rolled past Ron. Lying on it was James Brady, White House Press Secretary. James looked gray.

"Is he okay?" Ron asked the nurse.

She shook her head. "He was shot in the head. They don't think he's going to make it."

Right there and then, Ron prayed for James to be healed. Then he thought about the man who had shot at him and James. Ron did not believe that he could ask for God's help to heal James if he felt hatred for the shooter. He silently prayed that God would help the shooter to deal with his demons.

Moments later Ron breathed in anesthetic gas through the mask placed over his mouth and nose and quickly drifted from consciousness. Six hours later he awoke and again drifted off into unconsciousness.

The following day Ron heard the whole story of what had happened to him. Jerry had not broken his rib. Rather, Ron had been shot in the side by a bullet that ricocheted off the limousine. The bullet had been flattened by its impact with the car. As a result, it was shaped like a tiny Frisbee when it entered Ron's side between his ribs. The mark the bullet left on the outside of Ron's body was so small that the doctors didn't notice it at first, but the trail of damage it left inside his body was life-threatening. The bullet had ripped through Ron's left lung, collapsing it, and stopped less than an inch from his heart. The doctor told Ron that he had lost half the blood in his body before they were able to stabilize his condition.

Three other people had also been shot. James Brady, whom Ron had seen wheeled past on his way to surgery, was still in critical condition. A Washington police officer had been shot in the back, and a Secret Service agent was shot in the stomach. Both of them were expected to survive and make a full recovery. The shooter had been a student named John Hinckley Jr. He was found to be mentally ill and had come to Washington, D.C., to shoot the president so that a young movie star named Jodi Foster would take notice of him and possibly fall in love with him. When Ron heard this, he prayed even harder for Hinckley and his family.

Even though he had been struck by one of Hinckley's bullets, Ron found many things in the situation to be thankful for. When he arrived at George Washington University Hospital, most of the doctors on staff were upstairs having a meeting. As soon as word reached them that the president of the United States was in the emergency room, they all ran to help. Within ten minutes of arriving in the hospital, Ron had some of the top doctors in the world at his side tending him. This had undoubtedly helped to save his life.

Things were not yet completely fine, however. The following day and the day after, Ron's body raged with infection, and his doctors feared that he would develop pneumonia. They prepared themselves for the possibility that the president might die. However, with his strong constitution and the use of antibiotics, Ron eventually won the battle and began to recover.

Ron stayed in the hospital for two weeks, and although the staff would have liked to have kept him longer, Ron was ready to go home to the White House. A hospital bed was set up in the Lincoln bedroom at the White House, and a medical staff was assembled to take care of him once he arrived. Ron insisted on walking to the limousine as he left the hospital, and he waved to the gathered crowd. He knew that many people had been praying for him and hoping he would fully recover from his injury, and he was grateful for their concern and prayers.

Now five sitting American presidents—Abraham Lincoln, James Garfield, William McKinley, John F. Kennedy, and Ronald Reagan—were members in the tiny "club" that had experienced an assassin's bullet. Ron was humbled to know that he was the only one to have survived an assassination attempt. He later wrote in his diary, "Whatever happens now, I owe my life to God and will try to serve Him in every way I can."

Meeting the Challenge

Twenty-nine days after being shot, Ronald Reagan felt well enough to address the Congress. He had a message that he wanted them to hear, but first he thanked them for all their support during his recovery.

> I'd like to say a few words directly to all of you and to those who are watching and listening tonight, because this is the only way I know to express to all of you on behalf of Nancy and myself our appreciation for your messages and flowers and, most of all, your prayers, not only for me but for those others who fell beside me....

Ron then pulled a letter from his pocket. It was from a second grader in Rockville Center, New York.

Ron read it aloud. "I hope you get well quick or you might have to make a speech in your pajamas." The members of Congress laughed, and then Ron read on. "P.S. If you have to make a speech in your pajamas, I warned you."

After reading the letter, Ron went on to talk about the need to get spending and inflation in the country under control, to cut taxes, and to create jobs for millions of unemployed Americans. His speeches were always well-crafted and inspiring, but at this time Ron knew everyone was paying attention because of the assassination attempt. He knew that the time was right to push forward with his political agenda and bring Democrats as well as Republicans along with him. He began his concluding remarks with a quote from the poet Carl Sandburg.

"The republic is a dream. Nothing happens unless first a dream." And that's what makes us, as Americans, different. We've always reached for a new spirit and aimed at a higher goal. We've been courageous and determined, unafraid and bold. Who among us wants to be first to say we no longer have those qualities, that we must limp along, doing the same things that have brought us our present misery? I believe that the people you and I represent are ready to chart a new course. They look to us to meet the great challenge, to reach beyond the commonplace and not fall short for lack of creativity or courage. Someone you know has said that he who would have nothing to do with thorns must never attempt to gather flowers. Well, we have much greatness before us. We can restore our economic strength and build opportunities like none we've ever had before.

In July 1981 Ron fulfilled an election campaign pledge he had made by nominating Sandra Day O'Connor to be appointed as the first woman justice on the Supreme Court. The U.S. Senate unanimously confirmed her nomination. Ron was delighted to see a woman receive such an honor. He believed that many other women would follow in her footsteps.

The same day that Ron decided to nominate Sandra Day O'Connor for the Supreme Court, he had another important decision to make—how to respond to a threatened strike by members of the Professional Air Traffic Controllers Organization (PATCO). These men and women, employees of the Federal Aviation Administration (FAA), wanted a large salary increase and their hours of work reduced to thirty-two a week.

Ron had no argument with the union going through the proper channels to ask for a pay increase and reduced hours for its members. Having been the president of a union (SAG) himself, he knew that that was the job of a union—to look out for the interests of its members. Yet he also believed that this should be done through the process of negotiation and not simply through the threat of a strike. In this instance Ron would not tolerate a strike, because such a strike would be illegal. All federal employees sign an oath that, because they served the American public, they would not take part in a strike. Such an oath was necessary to prevent such workers as fire-fighters, prison guards, police officers, and air traffic controllers from walking off their jobs and thus endangering the public by their actions.

Despite this, on August 3, 1981, thirteen thousand air traffic controllers—seventy percent of all controllers in the country—did not show up for work. The strike was on.

Ron knew that this was not a time for weakness. Decisive action was needed in the face of an illegal strike. He called an immediate press conference in the White House Rose Garden at which he ordered the air traffic controllers back to work. He gave them forty-eight hours to show up for work or, he told them, they would be fired. Of course, Ron didn't really want to fire anyone, but he knew that the American people had voted for his no-nonsense approach to government, and this was his first test in a national emergency.

The members of PATCO seemed to think Ron was bluffing, because when the deadline passed, only about thirteen hundred of the thirteen thousand striking air traffic controllers had returned to work. Ron immediately asked the attorney general to remove those who had not returned to work from the federal payroll and asked the FAA to begin the process of training new air traffic controllers. In the meantime, the thirty percent of workers who had stayed on the job, plus those who had returned to work, and a contingent of military air traffic controllers controlled the nation's airways. This was Ron's first big test as president, and he was satisfied that he had made the right decision and that the people of the United States were behind him.

Meanwhile, Nancy was elevating the White House to a new level of elegance. Most people assumed that the presidential mansion was a luxurious place to live, but the reality was that many of the White House's rooms were rundown and needed updating. There were not even enough matching plates and cups to host a large state dinner. Every president and first lady put their stamp on their time in the White House, and the Carters had preferred simple meals and small parties. Nancy, though, with her Hollywood background, saw the White House as a glittering social hub. She enlisted personal friends to donate money to a fund to update things in the White House.

She also had another reason for her action. Since the assassination attempt, Nancy had become extremely concerned about Ron's safety. She made him wear a bulletproof vest when he went out in public, and she even had him wear a lead-lined raincoat over the vest if it was raining. It was much easier for the Secret Service to screen visitors coming into the White House than it was for them to check everyone around the president when he was out in public. This meant that Nancy was much more relaxed when Ron attended social events within the White House than events outside.

By Christmas 1982, the country was in much better shape. Only five percent of Americans were out of work, inflation had dropped from eighteen percent to eight percent, and the value of the stock market was soaring. America seemed to be getting back on its feet. Despite this, Ron and his administration had not been able to reduce government borrowing and balance the budget as they had promised to do. In fact, during President Carter's last year in office, the budget deficit had been $60 billion, but by 1984 it had soared to $175 billion a year. When all the debts the United States government owed were totaled, the figure amounted to $2.5 trillion dollars. The interest payments on this amount cost the government billions of dollars each year. Liberals complained that all this money should be going to the poor and needy, and they called for Ron to do more to help the most disadvantaged members of society.

Despite the growing budget deficit, most people in the United States agreed that they were better off than they had been for years. The American dream was still intact—people had jobs, money in the bank, and the opportunity to own their own homes.

While Ron concentrated on economic conditions at home, he also kept an eye on what was happening outside the United States. One place he kept a close eye on was the Soviet Union. The United States and the Soviets had been engaged in a cold war since the end of World War II. This cold war was an ongoing state of tension between the two countries, and included the buildup of nuclear bombs in both countries.

Ron was greatly concerned about this buildup of nuclear weapons, and in March 1983 he introduced the Strategic Defense Initiative (SDI). The aim of this initiative was to use ground and space-based weapons systems to defend the United States against a nuclear missile attack. The plan was quickly dubbed Star Wars. Ron and his administration hoped that it would create a balance of power that would deter the possibility of nuclear war. Congress allocated money to the military for the initiative, and plans were made to make Star Wars a reality.

In October 1983 Ron faced another foreign crisis, this one in the Caribbean. A radical Marxist group overthrew the left-leaning government of the island nation of Grenada, one hundred miles north of Venezuela. It executed the prime minister, Maurice Bishop. Present on Grenada at the time of the overthrow of the government was a contingent of Cuban military personnel and engineers, who were in the country to help build a large, new international airport. With the overthrow of Bishop's government and the presence of Cuban soldiers, an unstable and volatile political situation quickly developed on Grenada. The following week, a group of Grenada's Caribbean neighbors—Jamaica, Barbados, St. Vincent's, St. Lucia, Dominica, and Antigua—appealed directly to Ron for help in dealing with the situation on Grenada. They feared that it would not be long before the radical forces on the island backed by Cuba would be attacking their countries, overthrowing their governments, and replacing them with Marxist overlords.

Ron listened carefully to the argument the leaders of these countries put forth. Also, when he learned that eight hundred American students were studying at St. George's University Medical School in Grenada and could be in danger of being taken hostage, Ron decided he had to act. He ordered an American invasion of Grenada to rescue the students and restore civil order to the country.

On October 25, seven thousand American troops invaded Grenada. After several days of fighting in which nine American soldiers were killed and 116 were wounded, the United States secured the country and ousted the rebel government. By mid-December 1983, calm had been restored to Grenada, the island's constitution had been reinstated, and Grenada's governor general had put a new moderate government in place. With all of this achieved, Ron ordered the removal of American troops from Grenada.

In early 1984 Ronald Reagan had another big decision to make: should he run for a second term as president? He was nearly seventy-three years old and was already the oldest man to hold the office of president. He wondered whether Americans would reelect him at that age to a second four-year term.

Ron was torn as he pondered what to do. He was well past the age when most men retired, yet he felt that he had one last battle to win. During his four years in office, he had teamed up with British Prime Minister Margaret Thatcher to counteract the growth of Communism around the world. He called the Soviet Union an "Evil Empire," and he developed what had became known as the Reagan Doctrine to provide aid to anti-Communist resistance movements in Latin America, Africa, and Asia. U.S. military advisors had trained and equipped the mujahideen forces in Afghanistan as they fought off the Soviet occupation of Afghanistan.

Now, as Ron contemplated the idea of a second term in office, he wondered whether he could possibly lead the United States to a victory over Communism and the downfall of the Evil Empire, the Soviet Union. If he could do that, he decided, it would be worth a second term in office.

Chapter 19

Taking Action

It was Sunday, January 20, 1985, and Ron and Nancy stood side by side at the foot of the grand staircase in the White House where, in a private ceremony, Ron was sworn in for a second term as president. The following day was one of the coldest days on record in Washington, D.C., and all outdoor festivities were canceled. Instead, Ron celebrated his inauguration for a second term inside the Capitol Rotunda, where he repeated the oath of office publicly in front of government officials and friends and then gave his inaugural address.

The election process that won Ron a second term as president had gone fairly smoothly. Once Ron had decided to run again, the Republican Party nominated him as their presidential candidate, and Ron clearly had the majority of Americans behind him. He ran under the slogan that proclaimed, "It's Morning Again in America." When his Democratic opponent, Walter Mondale, tried to make Ron's age an issue in the race, Ron quipped, "I will not make age an issue of this campaign. I am not going to exploit, for political purposes, my opponent's youth and inexperience."

Most people seemed to agree with Ron that under his leadership the United States had become more prosperous and a proud nation once again. When the votes in the election were tallied, Ron had over fifty-four million votes, while Mondale received thirty-seven million. More important, Ron won the electoral college votes in forty-nine of the fifty states. His victory had been a landslide. Once again, George H. W. Bush would serve as vice president.

As he entered his second term as president, Ron thought he knew what lay ahead of him. But within weeks of taking the oath of office, a number of international crises presented themselves that required swift and decisive action on Ron's part.

The first situation Ron had to deal with came on March 10, 1985, with the death of Konstantin Chernenko, general secretary of the Communist Party of the Soviet Union and that nation's leader. Throughout his first term in office, Ron had tried to negotiate with the Soviets over reducing the number of nuclear missiles each country had. But his attempts to do this had been hampered by hardline Communist attitudes and by the death of three Soviet leaders within three years.

The following day the Politburo, the executive committee of the Soviet Communist Party, elected

Mikhail Gorbachev as the new general secretary of the Communist Party of the Soviet Union. At fifty-four years of age, Gorbachev was the youngest Soviet leader, and in him Ron saw an opportunity. Gorbachev seemed to embody new and fresh ideas about the place of the Soviet Union in the world. Ron immediately invited him to come to Washington, D.C., for a summit meeting regarding the reduction of nuclear missiles in both countries.

On June 14 Ron was awakened with the news that TWA flight 847, flying from Athens, Greece, to Rome, Italy, had been hijacked and flown to Beirut, Lebanon. Many of the passengers aboard the plane were American tourists, and the hijackers were demanding the release of Shiite prisoners being held in Israel in return for the lives of the passengers. The hijacked plane was then flown from Beirut to Algiers and then back again to Beirut. Along the way most of the women and children were released, as were most of the passengers who were non-Americans. Eventually thirty passengers—all Americans—were taken off the plane in Beirut and held as hostages.

Over a period of seventeen days, the hostage situation played itself out, with much behind-the-scenes negotiating by members of Ron's administration. Eventually the hostages were taken to Damascus, Syria, and released. In the course of the ordeal, the hijackers killed one hostage, a young American Navy diver. Americans recognized the hijacking as one more sign that the world was becoming more hostile toward them. Ron determined to stand firm against terrorists and any nations that plotted harm against the United States.

On July 11, 1985, Ron flew to Bethesda Naval Hospital in Maryland for his annual medical checkup. He was shocked to learn during the checkup that he had colon cancer. Immediate surgery was recommended, and the operation was performed the following day. It took surgeons three hours to remove two feet of Ron's colon.

When he awoke from the anesthesia, Ron was pleased to learn that the cancer had not spread. One doctor told him, "You have the insides of a forty-year-old!" At seventy-four years of age, Ron was cheered by the comment.

As Ron lay recovering in the hospital, Vice President Bush, White House Chief of Staff Don Regan, and several other White House aides came to confer with him. One of the things they updated him on was the plan that was taking shape in secret negotiations between the White House, the Israeli government, and a moderate but influential group in Iran. It was hoped that this plan would help to improve U.S.-Iranian relations. Under the plan, Israel would ship weapons to the Iranian group, who in turn would use their political influence within the Iranian government to try to achieve the release of six American hostages being held by terrorist groups in civil war–torn Lebanon, over which the Iranian government had some influence. The United States would then resupply the Israelis with weapons similar to those the Israelis had provided to the Iranians and would receive the Israeli payment for them. Ron asked a few questions about the plan to satisfy himself that it was sound and that if news ever leaked out about it, it would not appear that the United States was dealing arms for hostages.

Three months later, on October 7, 1985, Ron received a chilling briefing. Four men representing the Palestine Liberation Front (PLF) had taken control of a cruise ship, the *Achille Lauro,* off the coast of Egypt. The world waited to see what would happen next. The hijackers demanded the release of fifty Palestinians being held in Israeli prisons. To show that they were serious, the hijackers killed a wheelchair-bound passenger and threw his body overboard. The murdered passenger was Leon Klinghoffer, an American. Ron kept a close eye on the situation, and after two days of negotiations, the hijackers agreed to leave the ship if they were given safe conduct.

Because the incident with the *Achille Lauro* followed so closely on the heels of the hijacking of TWA flight 847, many Americans felt vulnerable in a way they never had before. As a result, many canceled their trips to Europe and concerned themselves with what might happen next to Americans.

Ron, however, was not happy with the outcome of the negotiations that had ended the hijacking of the *Achille Lauro.* He believed that the men who had killed Klinghoffer should not get off free but should stand trial for their crime. On October 10, as the four hijackers were being flown on an Egyptian commercial airliner to Tunisia, Ron ordered American fighter planes from the aircraft carrier USS *Saratoga* to intercept the Egyptian airliner and force it to land at a NATO base in Sicily, where the hijackers were arrested by Italian authorities. Some tense moments erupted afterward. Egypt demanded that the United States publicly apologize for forcing the airplane off course, and the Italians were not happy about the NATO airbase in Italy being used for the operation. Eventually the situation calmed down, and the four hijackers were tried and convicted in an Italian court for their actions.

The following month, Ron picked up a copy of *Time* magazine. The red and blue cover depicted his face on the left side and Mikhail Gorbachev's on the right. Above the pictures were the words "The Summit—Let's Talk" and "Geneva: The Whole World Will Be Watching." The featured article was about the upcoming summit meeting between Ron and the Soviet leader. Gorbachev had accepted Ron's offer to meet for a summit, but only if it was held somewhere other than Washington, D.C. Geneva, Switzerland, had been decided upon as the venue.

Ron read the *Time* magazine article, which did not sound an optimistic note. It read in part:

> Discussions preceding the summit have often seemed to highlight rather than narrow differences. On arms control, inevitably the main issue in a world living under a perpetual threat of nuclear extinction, the U.S. and U.S.S.R. have exchanged proposals that call for cutting to 6,000 the number of "nuclear charges" in their arsenals, but they differ deeply on what warheads and bombs to put in that category. Progress, if any is possible, awaits a decision by Reagan to agree to some limits on his

Star Wars defensive shield, or by Gorbachev to shoot for a deal without any such limits. On regional issues (such as Afghanistan and Central America) and human rights, the discussions amount largely to mutual accusations of meddling, subversion, repression.

It would be naive to expect the leaders of two nations with sharply contrasting political and social systems and deeply differing values even to begin to solve these impacted problems in eight hours of talks on Tuesday and Wednesday. But their meeting could at least set the tone for whatever combination of shouting and serious negotiation (it is unlikely to be either/or) will succeed the silence. A whole world will be anxiously watching every eyelid they lift or lower.

Ron had to agree that a strong possibility existed that the summit meeting would not be productive, but deep in his heart he felt otherwise. He sensed that the time was right for big changes in the relationship between the world's two superpowers, and he aimed to do everything possible to make that happen. It was the legacy he desperately wanted to leave behind when his term as president was over.

On November 19, 1985, the Geneva Summit began. Ron Reagan and Mikhail Gorbachev met each other for the first time and greeted each other warmly. The two leaders discussed the mutual distrust between the United States and the Soviet Union. Gorbachev harshly criticized Ron's Star Wars defense, but Ron stood his ground, telling the Soviet leader that given the extent of the mistrust between their nations, Star Wars was necessary. The two also bickered over human rights. Despite the hard talk that went on in the meetings, the summit ended cordially, and the two leaders agreed to meet again for another summit meeting in Reykjavík, Iceland, in October 1986.

Ron was encouraged by the outcome of the summit. He believed that developing a personal relationship with a leader was the first step to breaking down the tensions that existed between two countries. He thought that he had made progress in establishing that sort of relationship with Gorbachev. He hoped that as a result of the meeting Gorbachev would come to see that the United States really did desire peace above all else. The two leaders had agreed in principle that each of them would reduce his country's offensive nuclear weapons by fifty percent. All in all, it was an encouraging start, and Ron reported back to Congress on the summit: "While we still have a long way to go, we are heading in the right direction." Ron looked forward to making more progress at the next summit in Iceland.

On Tuesday, January 28, 1986, Ron was holding a briefing at the White House with his press secretary when several staff members burst through the door. "Mr. President, you have to come and see this. The *Challenger* space shuttle has exploded!"

The color drained from Ron's face as he hurried from the briefing room. One of the astronauts aboard the space shuttle was Christa McAuliffe, a civilian schoolteacher. Ron knew that millions of schoolchildren around the country would be tuned in to watch the launch on television.

The press office was next door. Every television monitor in the room was playing the same scene over and over. It was heartbreaking to watch but impossible to look away as the shuttle went through a flawless countdown and liftoff, followed by seventy-three seconds of perfect early flight. Then, all of a sudden, a large, white cloud engulfed the shuttle, with plumes of bright orange flame shooting out in all directions. The NASA commentator on the television was silent for a moment, and then he said, "We have a report from the flight dynamics officer that the vehicle has exploded."

At that moment Ron did not feel one bit like president of the United States. He felt like every other man and woman in the room as they watched seven fellow Americans engulfed in a fiery death. It was one of the hardest days of Ron's life, and he knew that as president he had to say something to try to help the nation accept what had happened. Ron's speechwriter, Peggy Noonan, helped him craft the words he wanted to say that night as he addressed the nation from his desk in the Oval Office.

First, Ron spoke to adults, and then he switched to the schoolchildren of America who had watched the tragedy live. "I know it's hard to understand, but sometimes painful things like this happen. It's all part of the process of exploration and discovery. It's all part of taking a chance and expanding man's horizons. The future doesn't belong to the fainthearted;

it belongs to the brave. The *Challenger* crew was pulling us into the future, and we'll continue to follow them."

Ron concluded the speech with the words, "The crew of the space shuttle *Challenger* honored us by the manner in which they lived their lives. We will never forget them, nor the last time we saw them, this morning, as they prepared for their journey and waved goodbye and 'slipped the surly bonds of earth' to 'touch the face of God.'"

Three days later, Ron and Nancy traveled to the Johnson Space Center in Houston, Texas, to speak at a memorial service honoring the dead astronauts. He told the assembled crowd of six thousand NASA employees, four thousand guests, and the families of the astronauts, "Sometimes, when we reach for the stars, we fall short. But we must pick ourselves up again and press on despite the pain."

Of all the duties Ron performed as president, by far the most difficult was the task of comforting the families of Americans slain in war or through tragedy. The death of seven astronauts aboard the *Challenger* was a particularly sad event for him. Ron knew there was not much he could say to the families of the dead astronauts except to remind them how heroic their loved ones were, and how these heroes had been willing to make sacrifices to reach their dreams.

As the year progressed, Ron faced many more instances in which he needed to reassure people with those words. On April 6, 1986, just nine weeks after the *Challenger* disaster, while vacationing at his ranch in the Santa Ynez Mountains of California, Ron was briefed on another tragedy, this time involving Americans overseas. A bomb had exploded at a disco nightclub in West Berlin, West Germany, frequented by U.S. servicemen and women. Two American soldiers and a Turkish woman had been killed outright in the blast, and a third serviceman was seriously injured. In addition, flying shrapnel had injured 229 other people, 79 of them Americans.

Slowly Ron learned more details of the attack. What he learned angered him. Intelligence officers reported that messages intercepted coming out of Libya clearly showed that the Libyan leader, Colonel Muammar Gaddafi, was responsible for the bloodshed in West Berlin.

Ron knew that this was not a time to blink. He told the American public, "When our citizens are attacked or abused anywhere in the world on the direct orders of hostile regimes, we will respond so long as I'm in this office." And respond he did. On April 15, 1986, nine days after the bombing in West Berlin, U.S. Air Force fighter-bombers were flying above Libya, targeting the capital, Tripoli, and the city of Benghazi. The main targets of the planes were the Libyan naval academy, the capital's military airport, and Libyan army barracks. Tripoli's embassy area and residential districts also suffered extensive damage. Although accurate figures did not reach the United States, three medical centers in Tripoli reported treating hundreds of casualties, many of them civilians. The American public saw television images of mobs of angry survivors in the streets

shouting, "Down, down USA. Death to all Americans." The situation was bad, and Ron was concerned that it could get worse. Yet in his mind he'd
had no other choice but to take direct action against
Libya.

October rolled around, and on October 11, 1986,
Ron and Mikhail Gorbachev sat down face-to-face
in Reykjavík, Iceland. The goal of this summit was
to come up with the basis of a treaty to limit the
number of intermediate-range nuclear missiles each
nation had. To the surprise of advisors on both sides,
Ron and Gorbachev agreed in principle to removing
all intermediate-range nuclear missiles from Europe
and limiting the number each country had to one
hundred nuclear warheads. The two also agreed to
a plan to get rid of all nuclear weapons by 1996, ten
years away.

When Gorbachev insisted that Ron scrap his
Star Wars defense shield, however, Ron once again
refused. As a result, the two men left the summit
having agreed on many things in principle but without a signed treaty, as they had hoped.

Although he was disappointed by the outcome
of the summit, Ron believed that the Soviet leader
would come around and see that signing a treaty
limiting nuclear weapons was in his country's best
interest, regardless of his opposition to Star Wars.

On November 26, 1986, news leaked out in the
press that the Reagan administration had been
secretly funding the Contras, anti-Communist gue-
rillas fighting the Communist Sandinistas in Nicara-
gua, and that the money to do this had come from

the sale of arms to Iran. Ron was as surprised as most Americans at this news. Of course, he knew about the secret deal for the Israelis to sell arms to Iran, in the hope that Iranian influence in Lebanon would lead to the release of American hostages there. But he had no idea that the profits from this sale of weapons had been directed to the Contras.

Supporting the Contras was in direct violation of U.S. law. Apart from money going illegally from his administration to the Contras, what frustrated Ron most about the situation was that he knew people would not believe him when he said he knew nothing of this action and that it was not authorized by him. Nonetheless, he was the president, and he accepted that regardless of what he knew about the situation, he would have to take full responsibility for the actions of people within his administration. That is what he did. Ron gave an address to the nation in which he stated that the weapons transfer to Iran had indeed occurred but that the United States had not traded arms for hostages, and he took full responsibility for the incident.

Despite Ron's address, what became known as the Iran-Contra scandal did not go away. The U.S. Congress began hearings into the incident, and Ron eventually appointed a three-man commission to investigate the issue as well. By March 1987, both inquiries were complete. Neither group found any evidence that Ron fully knew what was going on in the Iran-Contra scandal. However, fourteen administration officials were charged with crimes, and eleven of them were convicted.

In June 1987 Ron was in West Germany, where on June 12 he stood at the Brandenburg Gate in West Berlin to make a speech commemorating the 750th anniversary of the city. Standing with the Brandenburg Gate and the Berlin Wall that divided West Berlin from Communist East Berlin at his back, Ron laid out a challenge for Mikhail Gorbachev.

We welcome change and openness, for we believe that freedom and security go together, that the advance of human liberty can only strengthen the cause of world peace. There is one sign the Soviets can make that would be unmistakable, that would advance dramatically the cause of freedom and peace. General Secretary Gorbachev, if you seek peace, if you seek prosperity for the Soviet Union and Eastern Europe, if you seek liberalization, come here to this gate. Mr. Gorbachev, open this gate. Mr. Gorbachev, tear down this wall!

Six months later, in December 1987, Gorbachev was in Washington, D.C., for another summit with Ron. The Soviet leader had finally relented in his opposition to the Star Wars defense program. During the summit in the East Room of the White House, the two leaders signed the Intermediate-Range Nuclear Forces Treaty. The treaty eliminated nuclear and conventional ground-launched ballistic and cruise missiles. It had defined such missiles from the United States and Soviet arsenals as those with a flight range between three hundred and thirty-four hundred miles,

Ron was delighted that the treaty had been signed. By now he realized that he had just over a year of his presidency left, and he wanted every minute of that time to count. Unfortunately, one thing that eluded Ron and his administration was reining in the federal budget deficit. Throughout his presidency the budget had continued to grow, and economists were now warning that the U.S. economy might well collapse unless the government began to pay down the billions of dollars it owed in national debt.

Meanwhile, Ron and Nancy were both concerned about drug addiction in the United States. Law enforcement officers told Ron that most of the crime in the country could be linked to drug or alcohol use. Nancy took up the cause of promoting drug addiction prevention, coining the phrase "Just Say NO!" to drugs, which she hoped would help young Americans think twice before taking drugs.

The remainder of the year went by fast. Ron had more social issues to grapple with. The Senate announced a plan for combating a new and deadly disease—AIDS—that was reaching epidemic proportions in the country. Ron signed into law the Disaster Assistance Act, which provided federal aid to farmers affected by drought. He also signed into law the Fair Housing Act Amendment, outlawing private and public discrimination in housing. In September he signed the U.S.-Canada Free Trade Agreement. During this time, Ron also campaigned for Vice President George H. W. Bush, the Republican nominee to replace him as president.

In May 1988 Ron traveled to Moscow for one last summit meeting with Gorbachev. During the trip to Moscow, a journalist asked Ron whether he still considered the Soviet Union to be the "Evil Empire." "No," Ron said. "I was talking about another time, another era." While in Moscow, at the request of Mikhail Gorbachev, Ron made a speech at Moscow State University on free markets.

Ron was aware that his time was growing short when he broke ground for what would become the Ronald Reagan Presidential Library and Center for Public Affairs. The library was set up on a leveled-off hilltop in the Simi Valley, about forty miles northwest of downtown Los Angeles. It felt strange to Ron to be looking at the place where he would one day be buried. Ron hoped that before that happened, he and Nancy would enjoy many happy years of retirement together.

Chapter 20

Destiny at His Side

On January 11, 1989, Ronald Reagan sat in front of the television cameras in the Oval Office to give his final presidential address to the American people. He stared into the camera, cleared his throat, and began.

> My fellow Americans: this is the thirty-fourth time I'll speak to you from the Oval Office and the last. We've been together eight years now, and soon it'll be time for me to go. But before I do, I wanted to share some thoughts, some of which I've been saving for a long time.
>
> It's been the honor of my life to be your president....
>
> It's been quite a journey this decade, and we held together through some stormy seas.

And at the end, together, we are reaching our destination.

The fact is, from Grenada to the Washington and Moscow summits, from the recession of '81 to '82, to the expansion that began in late '82 and continues to this day, we've made a difference. The way I see it, there were two great triumphs, two things that I'm proudest of. One is the economic recovery, in which the people of America created—and filled—19 million new jobs. The other is the recovery of our morale. America is respected again in the world and looked to for leadership....

We cut the people's tax rates, and the people produced more than ever before. The economy bloomed like a plant that had been cut back and could now grow quicker and stronger. Our economic program brought about the longest peacetime expansion in our history: real family income up, the poverty rate down, entrepreneurship booming, and an explosion in research and new technology....

Common sense also told us that to preserve the peace, we'd have to become strong again after years of weakness and confusion. So, we rebuilt our defenses, and this new year we toasted the new peacefulness around the globe. Not only have the superpowers actually begun to reduce their stockpiles of nuclear weapons—and hope for even more progress is bright—but the regional conflicts that rack the globe are also beginning to cease. The Persian Gulf is no longer a war zone. The Soviets are leaving Afghanistan. The Vietnamese are preparing to pull out of Cambodia, and an American-mediated accord will soon send 50,000 Cuban troops home from Angola....

And so, good-bye, God bless you, and God bless the United States of America.

Nine days later, on January 20, Ron sat behind his Oval Office desk one last time. He pulled out a piece of stationary from the drawer with the words "Don't let the turkeys get you down!" printed across the top of it, and then wrote,

Dear George,

You'll have moments when you want to use this particular stationery. Well, go for it.

George, I treasure the memories we share and wish you all the very best. You'll be in my prayers. God bless you and Barbara. I'll miss our Thursday lunches.

Ron

Ron then placed the note in the top drawer of the desk.

Just then Colin Powell, Ron's national security advisor, entered the room. He had a grin on his face. "Mr. President, the world is quiet today."

As he looked out the window, Ron noticed that the weather was unseasonably mild. This was in stark contrast to the freezing temperatures that had stopped much of his official second inaugural celebrations four years earlier.

Ron's thoughts were interrupted by a group of photographers from the White House press office who were there to take a few last photos of him. And then it was time for Ron to go back upstairs to get Nancy and escort her to George H. W. Bush's inauguration.

Ron and Nancy sat in the back of the presidential limousine one last time as the motorcade made its way up Pennsylvania Avenue. They held hands and waved at the huge crowd who had gathered for the day of celebration. When the swearing-in ceremony was over, the new president, George H. W. Bush, and his wife, Barbara, walked Ron and Nancy through the Capitol Rotunda to the other side of the building where a military helicopter was waiting to whisk the Reagans away.

Ron knew that the rest of the day belonged to George Bush and his vice president, Dan Quayle. He was immensely proud to be part of the peaceful transfer of power from one president to the next. This was something Ron often reminded people that happened first in the United States and was at the heart of what America was all about.

Ron helped Nancy aboard the helicopter. Once they were seated, the craft slowly lifted off. Ron looked down at the sight below as the pilot circled the Capitol. He could see the cheering throngs of people crowded onto the mall and squeezed along the side of the streets the inauguration parade would follow.

Ron turned to Nancy and pointed down at the White House. "Look, honey, there's our little shack," he joked.

Nancy smiled back at him.

The helicopter pilot then set a course for Andrews Air Force Base, and before Ron knew it they had landed at Andrews. At the base Ron had one last opportunity to review the troops. This had always been one of his favorite duties as commander in chief, and he was delighted to do it one last time before leaving Washington, D.C., behind. The Air Force band played the national anthem as Ron and Nancy climbed the stairs to Air Force One for the flight across the country to California. The Reagans were going home.

At the end of Ron's presidency, Ron and Nancy had purchased a beautiful home in the Los Angeles suburb of Bel Air. Nancy was excited to give the new place her special decorative touch, while Ron looked forward to spending time back at Rancho del Cielo in the Santa Ynez Mountains.

In California Ron and Nancy's life settled into a happy pattern. Ron particularly enjoyed being free of the burden of worrying whether his presence would put others in jeopardy. After the assassination attempt, he had been advised to stop going to church and other public events that could not be properly screened for security. But now that he was a private citizen again, Ron resumed his Sunday churchgoing. He also loved to walk into a store to buy a gallon of milk or a birthday card without the area first having to be swept for bombs and guns.

214 Ronald Reagan: Destiny at His Side

On November 9, 1989, Ron received wonderful news. On June 12, 1987, he had stood before the Berlin Wall and declared, "Mr. Gorbachev, tear down this wall!" And on November 9, 1989, the East German government declared that East Germans were now free to cross the border into West Germany and West Berlin. Ron watched the television images as a huge crowd of East and West Berliners gathered at the wall to celebrate and then began to take sledge-hammers and break down the Berlin Wall. By October 3, 1990, the Berlin Wall was gone, along with the East's Communist government, as East and West Germany were reunited into a single, democratic country.

Not only had East Germany thrown off its old Communist government, but also many of the other Communist countries of Eastern Europe had done the same. Even the Communist government of the Soviet Union seemed about to collapse. The idea of confronting Communism and the Soviet Union had spurred Ron on to a second term as president. Now he was watching the fruit of his efforts come to pass as Communism was on the retreat in Eastern Europe and other parts of the world.

On November 4, 1991, Ron was the guest of honor at the opening of the Ronald Reagan Presidential Library. The magnificent mission-style building was set on one hundred acres of land atop a leveled-off hill in Simi Valley overlooking the Pacific Ocean. Inside, the Reagan Foundation had re-created many of the places and events that were turning points in Ron's personal and public life. It felt strange to Ron as he wandered through the exhibits. There was an old riding saddle he had used on Tar Baby, a portion of the Berlin Wall, and a replica of the Oval Office, complete with a jar of jelly beans, which Ron loved to eat while working in the office.

In the speech he gave at the opening of the library, Ron affirmed the principles his mother had taught him as a small child. "I know in my heart that man is good, that what is right will always eventually triumph, and that there is purpose and worth to each and every life."

Ron continued to make speeches and support candidates and positions that he believed in. He was particularly vocal about the president's being able to have the right to line-item (veto certain items in a bill that he disagreed with). He was also vocal about repealing the 22nd Amendment, which prevents a president from serving more than two terms as president. But the issue Ron was the most passionate about was a constitutional amendment that would require the government to balance the budget each year.

On April 27, 1994, Ron and Nancy attended the funeral of former President Richard Nixon. Four other U.S. presidents sat in the front row with Ron that day: George H. W. Bush, Jimmy Carter, Gerald Ford, and the current president, Bill Clinton. It was the first time this number of presidents had been gathered in one spot.

Ron did not know it at the time, but this would be his last public presidential appearance. Four months later he was diagnosed with Alzheimer's disease, which slowly destroys brain cells, confusing the patient and erasing his or her memories. Although Ron was eighty-three years old, his body was in such good physical shape that his doctors expected him to live for a long time. The Reagan family was devastated by the diagnosis, though they knew what to expect. They had seen Ron's mother, Nelle, suffer in a similar way.

Ron was concerned about how to get the information about his condition out to the public. In November 1994 he decided to be honest and upfront and wrote a farewell letter to the American people. It was perhaps the hardest letter Ron ever wrote. When it was complete, the text of the letter was released to the press. The letter read as follows:

My fellow Americans, I have recently been told that I am one of the millions of Americans who will be afflicted with Alzheimer's disease.

Upon learning this news, Nancy and I had to decide whether as private citizens we would keep this a private matter or whether we would make this news known in a public way....

So now we feel it is important to share it with you. In opening our hearts, we hope this might promote greater awareness of this condition. Perhaps it will encourage a clearer understanding of the individuals and families who are affected by it.

At the moment I feel just fine. I intend to live the remainder of the years God gives me on this earth doing the things I have always done. I will continue to share life's journey with my beloved Nancy and my family. I plan to enjoy the great outdoors and stay in touch with my friends and supporters.

Unfortunately, as Alzheimer's disease progresses, the family often bears a heavy burden. I only wish there was some way I could spare Nancy from this painful experience. When the time comes, I am confident that with your help she will face it with faith and courage.

In closing, let me thank you, the American people, for giving me the great honor of allowing me to serve as your president. When the Lord calls me home, whenever that day may be, I will leave with the greatest love for this country of ours and eternal optimism for its future.

I now begin the journey that will lead me into the sunset of my life. I know that for America there will always be a bright dawn ahead.

Thank you, my friends. May God always bless you.

Sincerely,
Ronald Reagan

With the release of Ron's letter, thousands of letters and cards poured into the Reagans' home in Bel Air. When he saw the ever-growing pile of letters and cards, Ron was glad that he had told the

American people about his situation. He knew that Nancy would need a lot of help and support to get through the difficult times that surely lay ahead.

Ironically, in his senior year at Dixon High School, Ron had written an essay for the school newspaper, the *Dixonian*, that included the words, "To every man comes Gethsemane! Some fight the battle surrounded by prison walls, but for all the soul is laid bare. Some fight the battle when old age is creeping on like a silent clinging vine." "A silent clinging vine" was an apt analogy of the disease that would slowly and relentlessly take over Ron's brain.

As the years rolled by, Ron became confused and disoriented. Sometimes he did not know where he was or to whom he was talking. He had to give up horseback riding and swimming, two of the things he loved the most.

In 1996 Ron's older brother Neil (Moon) died of heart failure, leaving Ron as the surviving younger brother.

Ron continued his decline into Alzheimer's disease, although he was able to take walks through the park and on the beach. Most of the time the people who recognized him just nodded and smiled but made no attempt to talk to him. Sometimes Ron even looked at photos of himself as president and asked who the tall man in the dark suit was. It broke Nancy's heart to have to tell Ron that he was the man in the photo.

Although Ron's mind had become feeble through disease, his heart and body remained healthy. But on January 12, 2001, he fell and broke his hip. He was taken to St. John's Hospital in Santa Monica, California, where he had surgery to repair the fracture. It was a particularly difficult time for the Reagan family. In a sad coincidence, Ron's older daughter, Maureen, had melanoma (skin cancer) and was fighting for her life two floors up in the same hospital at the same time. Maureen was too ill to be taken down to visit her father, and Ron was too ill to visit his daughter.

On February 6, 2001, Ron turned ninety. At the time only two other former U.S. presidents had lived longer: John Adams and Herbert Hoover. After Ron's ninetieth birthday, Nancy and the children decided that Ron should no longer go out in public or receive visitors except for immediate family. Nancy calmly and with dignity explained this to a television interviewer. "Ronnie would want people to remember him as he was," she said.

Ron's fractured hip eventually healed, but Maureen Reagan lost her battle with cancer and died on August 8, 2001. Ron was not able to comprehend her death.

Toward the end, Ron was bedridden and seldom opened his eyes as Nancy and a crew of nurses tirelessly watched over him. Ronald Wilson Reagan died quietly of pneumonia at his house in Bel Air, California, on June 5, 2004. He was ninety-three years old and had suffered with Alzheimer's for ten years.

Ron's body was taken from the house to a funeral home and then on to his presidential library, where the family held a private ceremony. Following the ceremony, the coffin was carried to the library lobby for Ron's body to lie in repose for two days. In that time, over one hundred thousand people filed past the coffin to pay their last respects to the former president.

The family and the country had had ample time to plan Ron's funeral arrangements, which were extensive. The man who had spent his life walking with destiny at his side had one more trip to make. On June 9, 2004, Ronald Reagan's body was flown from California to Washington, D.C., where Ron became the tenth U.S. president to lie in state in the Capitol Rotunda. In the day and a half that Ron's coffin was in the rotunda, 104,684 people filed past it.

President George W. Bush, the son of Ron's vice president, George H. W. Bush, declared June 11 to be a National Day of Mourning. International tributes and guests poured into Washington, D.C., from around the world.

June 11, 2004, was also the date of Ron's state funeral, conducted in the Washington National Cathedral. At the service, former British Prime Minister Margaret Thatcher, former Canadian Prime Minister Brian Mulroney, and both George Bush Sr. and Jr. gave eulogies. Mikhail Gorbachev, the former leader of the old Soviet Union, was a guest of honor at the service.

Following the state funeral, the hearse bearing Ron's body wound its way through the streets of Washington, D.C. Thousands of flag-waving Americans wept silently as it passed. Ron's body was then flown aboard Air Force One to California, where another service was held at the Ronald Reagan

Presidential Library before Ron's coffin was interred in the library grounds.

The coffin rests under a circle of cream-colored granite, with Ron's name and birth and death dates etched into a simple stone slab atop it. The only other words, etched into stone behind the grave, are a quote from the speech Ron gave when he opened the Ronald Reagan Library:

> I know in my heart that man is good, that what is right will always eventually triumph, and that there is purpose and worth to each and every life.

Brown, Mary Beth. *Hand of Providence: The Strong and Quiet Faith of Ronald Reagan.* Nashville: WND Books, 2004.

Buckley, William F., Jr. *The Reagan I Knew.* New York: Basic Books, 2008.

Devaney, John. *Ronald Reagan, President.* New York: Walker, 1990.

Edwards, Anne. *Early Reagan: The Rise to Power.* New York: Morrow, 1987.

Morris, Edmund. *Dutch: A Memoir of Ronald Reagan.* New York: Random House, 1999.

Reagan, Maureen. *First Father, First Daughter: A Memoir.* Boston: Little, Brown, 1989.

Reagan, Ronald. *An American Life: The Autobiography.* New York: Pocket Books, 1990.

Reagan, Ronald, with Richard G. Hubler. *Where's the Rest of Me?* New York: Karz, 1965.

Reeves, Richard. *President Reagan: The Triumph of Imagination.* New York: Simon & Schuster, 2005.

About the Authors

Janet and Geoff Benge are a husband and wife writing team with more than twenty years of writing experience. Janet is a former elementary school teacher. Geoff holds a degree in history. Together they have a passion to make history come alive for a new generation of readers.

Originally from New Zealand, the Benges make their home in the Orlando, Florida, area.